Praise for *Experience God as Your Provider*

Brian Kluth has long been a trusted leader and guide in the arena of financial stewardship. His speaking and writing have served countless Christians in many nations. *Experiencing God as Your Provider* is full of helpful insights and encouraging stories. I'm happy to recommend this book.

> —**Randy Alcorn**, bestselling author of *The Treasure Principle* and *Money, Possessions, and Eternity*

The biblical truths and true stories in Brian's book will help inspire anyone and everyone that God is their true Provider. If you or someone you know has any financial concerns about the future, this is a must-read book.

> —**Howard Dayton**, Founder/CEO of Compass, Cofounder of Crown Financial Ministries, and author of *Money and Marriage God's Way*

Brian Kluth is a well-respected financial teacher all over the world. In this book, Brian challenges us to explore the most important financial principle of all time: God is our Provider and we can fully trust in Him. This book will help anyone successfully navigate the turbulent waters of these unstable economic times.

> —**Dr. Andrés G. Panasiuk**, President of Global Freedom Concepts and former International VP of Crown Financial Ministries in Latin America

All financial security begins with understanding God as our faithful and certain Provider. Brian Kluth has demonstrated this in his own life and has been a consistent communicator of this reality in everything he has written and eve~~ ~~ he has given. ~~ ~~rse this book wholeheartedly!

> —**Ron Blue**, President Kingdom Advisors

Change your financial relationship forever . . . reading this book will bring you closer as a couple and get you on the same page in helping you understand how God is your ultimate Provider.

—**Scott** and **Bethany Palmer**, The Money Couple from ABC News and authors of *First Comes Love, Then Comes Money*

Brian Kluth is a superb communicator and models depending on God as his Provider. You will be personally inspired and challenged as you get a glimpse into the heart of this man of God through this book.

—**Dan Busby**, President, Evangelical Council for Financial Accountability (ECFA)

God has uniquely called and gifted Brian Kluth to help people discover that God is their true Provider. I have watched Brian personally live out this truth in his own life. This book will give biblical instruction, proven ideas, and personal inspiration to all who read it.

—**Wesley K. Willmer**, SVP of ECFA (Evangelical Council for Financial Accountability) and editor of *Revolution in Generosity*

The insights and stories in Brian's book will take your spiritual and financial life to a whole new level.

—**Lee Jenkins**, President of Lee Jenkins Financial Ministries, financial advisor, and bestselling author of *Lee Jenkins on Money*

*Finding Financial
Stability in Unstable Times*

EXPERIENCE GOD
AS YOUR
PROVIDER

BRIAN KLUTH
with Stan Guthrie

MOODY PUBLISHERS
CHICAGO

Edited by: Christopher Reese   Cover design: thedugandesigngroup.com
Interior design: Ragont Design   Cover image: Alamy.com #A39T9CT

Library of Congress Cataloging-in-Publication Data

Kluth, Brian.
 Experience God as your provider : finding financial stability in unstable times / Brian Kluth with Stan Guthrie.
    p. cm.
 Includes bibliographical references.
 ISBN 978-0-8024-4425-7
 1. Wealth--Religious aspects--Christianity. 2. Money--Religious aspects--Christianity. 3. Finance, Personal--Religious aspects--Christianity. 4. Trust in God. I. Guthrie, Stan. II. Title.
 BR115.W4K58 2010
 241'.68--dc22
                              2010014417

Moody Publishers is committed to caring wisely for God's creation and uses recycled paper whenever possible. The paper in this book consists of 30 percent post-consumer waste.

We hope you enjoy this book from Moody Publishers. Our goal is to provide high-quality, thought-provoking books and products that connect truth to your real needs and challenges. For more information on other books and products written and produced from a biblical perspective, go to www.moodypublishers.com or write to:

Moody Publishers
820 N. LaSalle Boulevard
Chicago, IL 60610

1 3 5 7 9 10 8 6 4 2

Printed in the United States of America

I dedicate this book to my Lord and Savior Jesus Christ.
Without His presence and His Word working
in my life, this book would not be possible.

I also dedicate this book to my wonderful wife, Sandi.
It has been her faith in God, contented spirit,
and generous heart that have allowed us to discover
and live out the truths in this book.

CONTENTS

INTRODUCTION

I have always appreciated the wisdom of the saying, "When all else fails, read the instructions."

We live in a time when lots of things are shaking and more and more things are failing. We are at a unique time in American history and our personal history when we need real help, real hope, and real answers for the day-to-day realities we're facing. We live in a financial and work world that is experiencing rapid and unprecedented changes.

Americans have spent years building financial houses that now resemble sand castles on the beach. For a long time many of our sand castles looked beautiful and kept getting bigger in the sunshine of the day. But strong ocean tides beyond our personal control are beginning to move in and our sand castles are beginning to crack and dissolve.

Jesus said in Matthew 7:24–27,

Everyone who hears these words of mine and puts them into practice is like a wise man who built his house on the rock. The rain came down, the streams rose, and the winds blew and beat against that house; yet it did not fall, because it had its foundation on the rock. But everyone who hears these words of mine and does not put them into practice is like a foolish man who built his house on sand. The rain came down, the streams rose, and the winds blew and beat against that house, and it fell with a great crash.

The truth is that we have not been hearing Jesus' words on finances, provision, and generosity in our churches. For many decades, most churches have been strangely silent about the 2,350 verses in the Bible on these subjects that affect our lives every day.

So, instead of building on the rock of God's Word, we've gone after trying to get a piece of the rock of the American dream. In recent decades, all the studies would show that Americans (including Christians) have built their lives on consumerism more than contentment, greed more than generosity, pleasure more than prudence, leisure more than labor, and debt more than diligent savings.

Our financial and career decisions haven't been guided by the Word of God, but more by Madison Avenue marketing, investment advisors, real estate agents, corporate pension plans, shopping malls, credit card companies, banks and mortgage lenders, car makers, the fashion industry, and government programs and policies. If we are honest with ourselves, we have to admit that strong ocean tides have begun to erode and crumble our houses of sand. It's as if we've built a financial house of cards and now someone is shaking the table.

In the book of Haggai, God's people had been extremely materialistic and had lived for themselves more than for God. So God began to shake the economic system and reduced their ability to make money. He knew they had gotten their priorities all out of alignment, and He wanted to get their attention to help them to refocus on the Word of God, to reconsider their financial practices, and to realign their financial priorities so they would begin to put

God first in their lives again. Here's what the Scripture says in Haggai 1:3–11:

> The word of the Lord came through the prophet Haggai: "Is it a time for you yourselves to be living in your paneled houses, while this house remains a ruin?" Now this is what the Lord Almighty says: "*Give careful thought to your ways.* You have planted much, but have harvested little. You eat, but never have enough. You drink, but never have your fill. You put on clothes, but are not warm. You earn wages, only to put them in a purse with holes in it." This is what the Lord Almighty says: "*Give careful thought to your ways.* Go up into the mountains and bring down timber and build the house, so that I may take pleasure in it and be honored," says the Lord. "You expected much, but see, it turned out to be little. What you brought home, I blew away. Why?" declares the Lord Almighty. "Because of my house, which remains a ruin, while each of you is busy with his own house. Therefore, because of you the heavens have withheld their dew and the earth its crops. I called for a drought on the fields and the mountains, on the grain, the new wine, the oil and whatever the ground produces, on men and cattle, and on the labor of your hands." (emphasis added)

As a nation, we have been living a materialistic, me-first lifestyle for a long time. We have been putting money in our pockets (sometimes lots of money), but our pockets have had holes in them and we wonder where all of our money has gone. And now in the sovereignty of God, He has allowed cold winds to blow over our economy, and the values of our homes have gone down, our investments have shrunk, our paychecks have frozen or decreased, and our pension funds (if we have any) are at risk.

This book was written to help you "give thought to your ways" and to consider God's Word and God's ways. God wants you to see and experience Him as your Provider. God wants you to build your finances and life on the solid rock of His Word. God wants you to learn to become a generous person, and He wants to bring you help and hope for your faith, finances, family, and future. This book is filled with Scriptures that will instruct you and true stories that will inspire you. This is not a money management book, but rather a book that will help you manage your life under the *Lordship* of Christ.

PART ONE
Recognize God's Provisions

Chapter 1

YOUR JOB

Several years ago I did an all-day seminar in Eastern Europe for about a hundred people. The seminar was about what the Bible teaches regarding finances, provisions, and generosity.

After the seminar an older man came up to me and told me that for the first time in his entire life he heard the truth. I asked him what he meant. He replied,

For many decades our country was a communist country. During these years we were told that the government owned everything and that the government would provide for all of our needs. But this didn't work. Then communism fell and many people came to our country and told us about capitalism.

They taught us that we were the owners of our own possessions and destiny and that we needed to take care of our own needs. But for most people, this has not worked. Today, I learned about Christianity. You have taught me that God is the true Owner of all things, that we are to serve the Lord, honor Him with our lives, share whatever He gives us, and that God will be our Provider.

For this man, communism was a lie, and he felt that capitalism was a half-truth that only worked for some. But Christianity is true and works for everyone who is willing to follow Christ and His Word.

You see, the great news is that God is bigger than nations, economies, stock markets, currencies, and job markets. When we begin to understand this we don't have to live in fear but we can live in faith in a God who can provide for us in good times, bad times, and the in-between times.

If you work for a company, it is your employer, but God is your true Provider. What would you rather have in life—what your company can pay you or what God can provide for you? And I don't mean this in a skewed way that relies on a greed-based prosperity gospel message. I mean it in a way that helps you understand God as your heavenly Father who cares about your needs (not your greeds!), who can show His love for you and provide for you.

Let me explain the idea of God's ownership in our work world in another way. My friend Shari works for a bank, and the bank was recently bought by Wells Fargo and billionaire Warren Buffett. Understandably, in these uncertain economic times, this new ownership made the employees nervous. And why not? Everyone thinks that Buffett owns Wells Fargo, and no one knows what he may do to make Shari's bank more profitable. Like many company leaders focused on the bottom line, he may decide to cut staff, reduce benefits, and close some departments or branches.

We've all become accustomed to downsizing, or "right-sizing," after one company buys another. This is an unavoidable fact of life in our capitalist society. It's an old story, one that many of us are familiar with. Big fish eat smaller fish. The new owners get to call the shots because they have put up the capital and thus have earned the right to put good workers like Shari onto the street of if they want in pursuit of a healthier bottom line.

There's only one problem with this scenario. Warren Buffett does not own Wells Fargo. I'll acknowledge that Buffett may invest the money, place his own hand-picked team into Wells Fargo's management, bring in new bosses, lay off office workers, and have his own special parking spot in the Wells Fargo lot. But he does not actually own the company, nor do its shareholders. This question about "Who owns Wells Fargo and who is Shari's real boss?" isn't about communism, socialism, or capitalism. It isn't a political question, a social question, or even an economic question. It's a theological question—and a basic one at that. Warren Buffett, you see, for all his business skill and prowess, is merely a temporary steward of Wells Fargo and of all the bank employees. He is a manager of what God has entrusted to him during his lifetime. A steward manages the wealth of someone else, not his or her own. A steward will also be held responsible for how well he managed the owner's assets. Warren Buffet is ultimately responsible to God for what he does with the Lord's resources and the people who are entrusted to him during his lifetime.

Warren Buffett is a temporary steward, because he does not own Wells Fargo. Who does? Why, God, of course! Ultimately, God

> *If you work for a company, it is your employer, but God is your true Provider. What would you rather have in life, what your company can pay you or what God can provide for you?*

is the Provider and the Owner of ALL things in life. We work and plan and produce from what God provides for us, but ultimately it all goes back to God, because He holds the deed. This truth hasn't changed, and it won't change. It has been that way, it is that way, and it will continue to be that way. As the Bible says, "The world is mine and all that is in it" (Psalm 50:12). People—you and me, and even the Warren Buffetts of this world—are only temporary stewards.

Of course, being a steward isn't bad news—at least not for the Christian. It's extremely good news. That's because Christian stewards are taken care of by the Owner of all. God is not a miser seeking to hoard everything for His own benefit, but a Giver, a Sharer, a Provider.

Getting back to Shari and Wells Fargo, we can trust the God who ultimately owns the bank to faithfully care for His stewards—not because He has to, but because He wants to. The Owner, you see, is also a Father. And fathers provide for their children. God is both the ultimate Father and the ultimate Provider for those who put their trust in Him. No wonder Jesus says, "If you, then, though you are evil, know how to give good gifts to your children, how much more will your Father in heaven give good gifts to those who ask him!" (Matthew 7:11).

THE PROVISION OF EMPLOYMENT

So if our Father is also our Provider, how does God provide out of His limitless wealth for His children? Well, for most people at most times, Provision No. 1 is our employment—what we do to produce income for our daily bread. God's main provision for our lives, for most of us, comes through our work. Sometimes, of course, after a bad day at work or wrestling with our vocational call, we're tempted to wonder whether we really want this provision. Work is, well, work. We sometimes come home tired, sore, or discouraged from our jobs. We think that work is part of the curse that flowed to humanity because of our sinfulness. Didn't God say to Adam, "By the sweat of your brow you will eat your food" (Genesis 3:19)? But if we back up in Scripture to the beginning, we discover that "the Lord God took the man and put him in the Garden of Eden to work it and take care of it" (Genesis 2:15). In a perfect environment, with a perfect Boss, Adam and Eve were created by God to be productive—to be fruitful. Since work existed in Paradise before the curse, it cannot be intrinsically evil. In fact, as the main portion of God's provision for us, it is inherently good. Yes, the fall has made work difficult, but the Father's redeemed children have the opportunity to see their work redeemed as well.

I am often asked to do guest preaching and seminars in churches around the country. During my message, I will often ask people to raise their hands if they get a paycheck from a company or organization. I then like to remind everyone that whoever gives them their paycheck is *not* their provider, but their employer. God may use an employer to help provide much of what you need in life, but God is so much bigger than your employer. I also encourage people to see that when they give financially to God as their highest financial priority that they are declaring to themselves and to the Lord that God is their Provider. Think about it. What would you rather have in life—what a company can pay for you or what God can provide for you? God is so much bigger than a paycheck, a pension, a company position, the stock market, and even our economy. Since He owns everything, He can provide the very things you need in life.

So, while God will use our employment to provide, He is not limited to what your company can do for you. But while we work for our employer, we need to be the best employee we can be while realizing that God is our ultimate Provider.

Work was part of Adam's life before the fall and after the fall. Work will be part of your life in this world and the world to come. If we go back to Adam's job resume, we discover that the oldest profession in the world is that of zoology. The Bible says that the

Lord God formed out of the ground all the beasts of the field and all the birds of the air. He brought them to the man to see what he would name them; and whatever the man called each living creature, that was its name. So the man gave names to all the livestock, the birds of the air, and all the beasts of the field (see Genesis 2:19–20). As God's steward, Adam was to lead, rule over, and bring order to God's creation. So his first task was to give names to all the livestock, the birds of the air, and the beasts of the field.

God provides the work. He also provides us with the ability to do the work. Psalm 90:17 is a great illustration of this principle. First the psalmist says, "May the favor of the Lord our God rest upon us." This is a sensible outlook. We need God's favor for everything, of course—our families, our ministries, our health, our relationships. But in this discussion, we focus on the fact that we need God's favor for the work He provides. The psalmist's wish quickly turns into a request, a prayer: "Establish the work of our hands for us—yes, establish the work of our hands."

When we understand that we are working for and with God instead of working for a paycheck, our whole attitude will change. I know of one woman who worked in a dirty factory. For many at her company their jobs were sheer drudgery. But when someone at church asked her what she did for a living, she replied, "I am a Christian serving the Lord to reach people with the love of God in my factory. But God has disguised me as a third shift welder to get me around the people He wants me to reach for Him." Wow! What a great attitude and perspective.

So, no matter where God places us, He can use us and He can provide for us.

May we all pray to God, "Establish the work of our hands." A lot of people approach life this way: "I'm going to major in a lucrative field, get a high-paying job, and be successful. With my money I'm going to buy all I want. I'll put my kids into the finest schools, buy a vacation home, and retire early." They think, like the rich man in Jesus' parable, that life consists in the abundance of their possessions. Then, like so many in our uncertain economic times, they lose it all, and someone else gets what they have worked so hard for. When *we* try to establish the work of *our* hands, we will fail—if not materially, then spiritually. Failure comes when we stewards take God's provision and act as if we own it and can dispose of it as we wish.

Don't ever go to work just for the money. Don't work for a paycheck; work for God. Paychecks come and go, but God remains, and only He can establish the work of our hands. Does this mean that only those in "full-time Christian service"—pastors and missionaries, mostly—can work for God? Not at all! God has created all of us with unique gifts, talents, skills, and opportunities. As Ephesians 2:10 notes, "For we are God's workmanship, created in Christ Jesus to do good works, which God prepared in advance for us to do." This encouragement is not just for pastors and missionaries—though they get to rejoice in it too—but for every Christian. We all have been created specifically by God to do specific good works, and many of them come in and through our work.

> *When we understand that we are working for and with God instead of working for a paycheck, our whole attitude will change.*

To do those good works, we need to pursue things that glorify God and bring blessing to others, knowing He has prepared us to do them. Work is not about a paycheck—though a paycheck may be involved. Work is about finding and following through on God's unique vocational calling in our lives.

I realize that some people might think, if it's not about doing anything just to get a paycheck, how will we survive? We have obligations and responsibilities for ourselves and others. We need food, shelter, and clothing, at a minimum, and our hectic twenty-first-century society tries to convince us we need a whole lot more. If our primary commitment is to focus on glorifying God and serving others—what we can give rather than what we can get—how will we meet our legitimate needs and responsibilities? Who will look out for us?

Again, remembering that God is our Provider allows us to do what others consider to be impossible. Jesus put it simply: "But seek first his kingdom and his righteousness, and all these things will be given to you as well" (Matthew 6:33). The question is not whether God will bring His provision into our lives, but whether we have the faith to believe it—and act upon it.

Let me explain how this works—or, at least, how it's worked in my life. When I first came to know Jesus Christ as my Savior and Lord as a college student, I was bartending in a nightclub to make money. After I became a Christian, I realized that what I was doing was not pleasing to the Lord and it certainly wasn't beneficial to our customers. I needed the money, but I wasn't comfortable doing what I was doing. So, I prayed about what to do and sought the counsel and prayer of godly people I knew. Ultimately, I turned in my resignation even though I didn't know what would happen next or how I would make the money I needed to live on.

After I resigned the Lord led me to return to my hometown and provided a better job with a company that allowed me to honor God and serve others in a positive way in my life. When I made the decision to resign, I was declaring to myself and the Lord that He was going to be my Provider and that I would look to Him to lead me and guide me. Proverbs 3:5–6 exhorts, "Trust in the Lord with all your heart and lean not on your own understanding; in all your ways acknowledge him, and he will make your paths straight." I was on a crooked path and God helped make my paths straight.

While making a decision to honor God is not always easy, I can testify to the truth of Philippians 4:19, which says, "And my

God will meet all your needs, according to his glorious riches in Christ Jesus." Therefore we can pray with confidence, "God, establish the work of our hands."

ADDITIONAL INCOME

God our Provider has a plan to allow us to glorify Him and bless others. He promises to meet our needs as we labor in those things to which He has called us. Many times He provides through a regular paycheck. Sometimes He provides us with extra work or income. We might get a raise, a commission, a bonus, overtime pay, freelance work, a home business, refunds, or rebates. These blessings, just as much from the hand of God as our regular employment, seem to be serendipitous extras, to spend as we please. We forget that God has brought even these extras into our lives, and they belong to Him. As Deuteronomy 8:17–18 says, "You may say to yourself, 'My power and the strength of my hands have produced this wealth for me.' But remember the Lord your God, for it is he who gives you the ability to produce wealth."

Every financial blessing in life comes from God. It's God's blessing, God's resource, God's kindness, and God's mercy. Yes, it can be used to benefit you, but perhaps God wants to do something else with it. Not long ago I was having breakfast with someone who was visiting from England. At the end of the breakfast we stood to leave and he said, "God is prompting me to give you $100," and he gave me a $100 bill. Imagine that! Someone handing you an unexpected $100 bill because God told him to do so. What would you do with an unexpected and extra $100? Before I could even think about how I was going to use this money, the Lord spoke to my heart and said, "This isn't for you, this is for someone else." So I immediately told the man from England, "Thank you for this gift, but I want you to know that this isn't for me. Someone else needs this more than I do, so I'm just going to keep it in my wallet until God shows me that person.

> *We need to learn to be open-handed in this tight-fisted world.*

Somewhere along the way I'm going to give this to someone and I will tell them that God had a man in England give this to me so that I could give this to them to meet a special need in their life."

After carrying the $100 bill in my wallet for a number of weeks, I met a new couple at church one Sunday who had just moved from another state. They had two little children and a car, but they had no money, no job, no home, and no food. God immediately prompted me, "This is the couple, give them the $100." I did and they were helped and blessed. Others in our church also showed them the love of Christ in tangible ways, and today they are active members in our church family.

Sometimes God brings us extra financial blessings not to heap them into our life, but so that they might flow through us. In other words, we need to learn to be *open-handed* in this tight-fisted world. In his book *The Treasure Principle*, Randy Alcorn says, "God does not always raise our income so that we can increase our standard of living, but rather increase our standard of giving."

Once, after I finished preaching a message on what the Bible teaches on finances and giving, a man came up to me with tears in his eyes. I asked him, "What's wrong?" He said, "Brian, all the days of my life I've been so proud of myself and my money-making abilities. I could squeeze money out of a rock. I've been great with money. But for the first time, I realize that my strength to make money comes from God. I'm seventy years old, and I never realized that God was the source of that strength. My life and my giving will be different starting today." That day this man learned what it meant to become open-handed in a tight-fisted world.

Shortly after my self-published *40 Day Spiritual Journey to a More Generous Life* Bible devotional became an unexpected bestseller with 100,000 copies in print in just nine months, the NBC affiliate in my town called me, to do a news story about the book. When they came to my house to interview me the reporter asked, "So, do you think God wants everyone rich?" I said, "No, I don't believe that." She said, "Well, then, what do you believe?" I said, "I believe that God wants everyone to learn to become more generous with whatever God entrusts to them—whether they have little or much." She then asked, "But didn't this bestselling book make you rich?" I said, "No, it helped make us more generous!"

Just because we made a lot more money from the book sales didn't mean God wanted us to spend this extra money on ourselves. My wife, Sandi, and I realized that God had given us more because there was more He wanted us to give to advance His kingdom.

No situation is too difficult for our Provider. A friend of mine in Georgia recently lost his job. He was well-known and respected in his industry. But a new CEO was named and almost overnight the new CEO eliminated my friend's position and his entire department and outsourced all their duties to an outside vendor. After twenty-six years of faithfully serving this organization, my friend and many of his colleagues were out on the street. Just like that, his job was gone. I knew this was rough for him, and I kept in touch by email and phone. A year after he lost his job, I was in his town on a business trip and we got together for breakfast. He told me with wonder in his voice, "My job is gone, but God is not. God has provided. He's provided side jobs, consulting income, and my wife's employment to help meet our needs during this time. I've actually made more money this year than I've ever made in my life. I'm enjoying doing some things that I never had time to do."

Another friend of mine unexpectedly lost his job and told me over lunch one day, "I made less money the year I was let go than I have made in years. I have a stay-at-home wife and five young daughters. But God provided for us again and again, even when we didn't have any regular income. During the time I was out of work, we learned that God was our true Provider."

Of course, God can also establish our work by putting us in a position to succeed and then enabling us to do so. As Psalm 75:6–7 (TLB) says, "Promotion and power come from nowhere on earth, but only from God. He promotes one and deposes another." The truth of this verse litters the pages of the Bible, which are filled with accounts of unlikely heroes and leaders who receive promotions to positions of great power and responsibility. Moses, a murderer and fugitive, rises to lead God's people out of bondage. Joseph, left in a pit by his jealous brothers, is named Egypt's second-in-command and saves the nation from famine. Daniel, a mere Jewish exile, earns the respect of a pagan emperor and becomes a government official.

God can do the same for us. Note that the verse does not say that our *supervisors* promote and empower us. Sometimes we feel we are at the mercy of our boss, who can be good or bad as a people manager. I'm not minimizing the fact that human relationships are important at work, but our Provider works in, through, and sometimes around them to accomplish His will. Our work relationships can be sticky and sometimes go in the wrong direction, but ultimately a sovereign God rules over these matters and places us where He wants us to be. Our Provider is our Promoter. When we realize that God has called us to do a job, we can experience peace, no matter what the office politics are.

Once I was in northeast India teaching a seminar and I mentioned the Bible was against bribery. Some Christians in the audience told me, "You don't understand. Here in India that's how we do it. Bribery is how you get a job." When I explained God's Word, they replied, "You're an American; you don't understand. This is how we do it in India." I asked, "What do you mean?" They said, "Well, if a government job comes open, usually thousands of people apply for it. The only way to move your name up the list is to bribe somebody."

What could I say that would convince them? This was how it worked in that part of India. Then an older gentleman, about seventy years old, raised his hand and asked, "May I come forward?" Everybody became quiet as he took the microphone. The gentleman was a well-known, high-ranking government official. "How many of you know that I've been in government service all my life?" he asked. All the hands went up. Then he said, "All my life I've been asked, 'Who did you pay? How much did you have to pay them to get your positions and promotions?' I stand before you today to say that I have never paid anyone one rupee for my position. God has placed me where He wanted to place me. God must be your Source. He must be your Provider."

No one said a word. They could push back against the American, but not against this senior saint, who quoted this verse: "He promotes one and deposes another." God is the Promoter and Provider.

Yes, the workplace can sometimes be a difficult place of testing, of struggle, of failure. Even our best, most faithful efforts sometimes miss the mark, and no job is completely secure. Some of us feel hopeless, particularly those who have lost their jobs or fear that they might. It is to them that God says, "I know the plans I have for you . . . plans to prosper you and not to harm you, plans to give you hope and a future" (Jeremiah 29:11).

One day a woman at my church in Milwaukee, a mother on welfare, asked for some money so she could rent an apartment. I said, "If we give you the money, what's going to happen next month?" She said, "I can't worry about next month." I asked, "But do you have any work?" She answered, "No, I haven't worked in years. I don't have any skills. I've always been told I'm worthless and that I'm no good." I replied, "Yes, you need money, but you need more than that. You need to see that you have dignity. You have worth. God created you."

We gave this woman who thought so little of herself a computerized career test from Crown Financial Ministries that explores people's values, skills, passions, and experiences. After getting the results, this woman had an epiphany. She looked up and exclaimed,

"I'm valuable! I'm worth something! I have skills, I have abilities, and I can do something with my life." Within two weeks this woman had a job in a field that fit who she was. In two months she was off welfare and food stamps. Why? Because suddenly she understood that God had created her and that she could glorify God and bless others. She understood for the first time that she is "fearfully and wonderfully made" (Psalm 139:14), and she praised her Provider and Promoter.

Understanding that God is the Source of every good thing, including our work and the ability to do it, so will we.

For groups, classes, or family discussions, choose the most interesting three to five questions to discuss together.

1. When you were a child or in your teen years, what was a job or career you wanted to have when you grew up?
2. What type of work and responsibilities were you doing ten, twenty, or thirty years ago?
3. What has been some of the most satisfying work or volunteering you've ever done?
4. If you ever lost a full-time job, share any special ways God provided for you during this time.
5. In this chapter, we said that a company is not your provider, but your employeer. God is your true provider. When people grasp this truth, what difference do you think it will make in their life?
6. Do you feel God has "placed" you in your current position? If so, what are some reasons you feel God has placed you in this role?

EXPERIENCE GOD AS YOUR PROVIDER

Chapter 2

YOUR UNEXPECTED
PROVISION

In the first chapter, we examined how God owns everything, how He is our Provider, and how His ordinary provision for us, most of the time, is through our regular employment. But we also caught glimpses of how He sometimes works in extraordinary ways to deliver His resources to His children in need.

A friend testified that even after being laid off after working at one company for twenty-six years, God supplied his needs. But can we count on Him to do the same for us? Since God owns and controls everything, He is not limited to providing for us through a regular nine-to-five job (or, more likely these days, an eight-to-six, or for some people seven-to-seven or more). Believing that He is so limited betrays an unbiblical, secular worldview. In our society,

> *Sadly, even many professing Christians are "practical atheists" when it comes to their ability to believe that God can provide.*

many people do not believe or expect God can provide in tangible ways beyond their paycheck. Some people feel that even if God does exist, He cannot break into our clockwork world with power or provision. But this is not the God of the Bible. Sadly, even many professing Christians are "practical atheists" when it comes to their ability to believe that God can provide. Even Jesus' disciples questioned the Lord's ability to provide for thousands of people when they could only scrape together five loaves and two fish from a little boy's lunch box! If we want to progress in our understanding of God as our Provider, we will have to unlearn this mind-set—and quickly. One way to do it is to expect Him to do the unexpected.

In this context, that means that God can and sometimes will provide unexpected income or money to His faithful stewards. By unexpected I mean it was not necessarily money you were counting on receiving—you didn't earn it or deserve it; it showed up, and you just knew that somehow God was behind it. Isaiah 45:3 tells us about a God who thinks, and acts, outside the secular box: "I will give you the treasures of darkness, riches stored in secret places, so that you may know that I am the Lord, the God of Israel, who summons you by name."

Why does God pull back the curtain on these resources and give them to us? The answer is simple: "So that you may know that I am the Lord, the God of Israel, who summons you by name." Sometimes God just says, "I want to bless you, encourage you, help you, and let you know that I am aware of your needs."

This "unexpected provision" can be received in very personal ways with the timing so exact that you know that God was in it.

Once my wife, Sandi, and I were planning on going on a short-term missions trip to South America for a number of weeks. We sent out letters inviting people to help underwrite the cost of this ministry trip and we received very few responses and did not have enough money to go. As we prayed about what to do, we had a sense that God was going to provide in a different way than He had for some of our ministry trips in the past. One day we received a letter from the school district where Sandi had taught about ten years earlier. The letter explained that she had unused retirement dollars in an account that we didn't even know existed. We were told we could have all the funds in the account if we wanted them. So, we said yes, and these funds helped cover most of the cost for this ministry trip. For ten years this "treasure" sat in a dark place, waiting for the very time when we would need it for a ministry trip to South America. We discovered there really are "treasures of darkness" and "riches stored in secret places."

A number of years ago we were part of a church plant in Milwaukee. God blessed this new church and it kept growing and growing. We started out in a YMCA aerobics room that we quickly outgrew. We then moved to a ten-screen movie theater complex where we continued to grow. We then were presented with the God-given opportunity to buy a $2.2 million racquetball club building that we could convert into a church. All we had to do was come up with $500,000 in cash in ninety days and we could have it (at almost 80 percent off the asking price)! There was just one problem: We didn't have the money and saw little prospect of acquiring it. Most people in the church were blue-collar and young no-collar workers. We had ninety days to come up with half a million dollars. So one Sunday I taught our congregation about Isaiah 45:3 and God's ability to give "treasures of darkness" and "riches stored in secret places."

"That's the stupidest thing I've ever heard," Mike, a congregant who worked in a meatpacking plant, said afterwards. "What do you want me to do? Go to my hundred-year-old house and pull up the floorboards and look for money? Do you want me to break holes in the plaster wall and see if I can pull out some money? Where are treasures of darkness going to come from? Where are the riches stored in secret places? That's the stupidest thing I've ever heard! I can't even believe you told us about that verse."

Taken aback, I quickly replied, "Mike, all I said was to keep your eyes open. In this ninety-day miracle time, we don't know where all the money is going to come from. We don't know how it's going to happen. We just know we have ninety days to purchase this building for cash."

One day during those three months I got a call from Mike. "I need to tell you a story," he said. "I was in the factory working. The foreman opens the door, and he yells out into the shop, 'Michael, get in here!'

"Brian, do you know what that means?" Mike continued. "At our factory, we call this the 'death march' for people who are getting fired or laid off." He went on, "I started walking across the factory floor and I'm terrified. What am I going to do? How am I going to pay my bills? How am I going to take care of my family if I get fired or laid off today? I get to the foreman's office and he yells, 'Sit down,' and he hands me an envelope. I know it's a pink slip and I sit there, immobilized. The foreman says, 'Well, open it!' So I open it. It's not a pink slip; it's a check for $500. I didn't know what this was, so I asked the foreman, 'What is this, a severance check?' The foreman just said, 'You're doing a good job. It's a bonus. Now get outta here and get back to work.'"

Stunned, Mike walked out holding this check, and started thinking about all the ways he could spend it. Then Mike told me, "Brian, I heard God speaking in your voice: 'treasures of darkness,' 'riches stored in secret places so that you may know that I am the Lord who calls you by name.' Brian, I'd never heard of anyone at my factory getting a bonus from the foreman. All I've heard of is people getting fired and laid off when they did the death march. That verse is really true. God really can show up. God really can provide. If He can do that in my life, Brian, we're going to get that building!" Mike signed the back of the $500 bonus check over to the church so that he and his family could be part of the ninety-day miracle!

On the ninetieth day of our miracle journey, our church—made up of blue-collar and no-collar twenty- to thirty-year-olds—handed the bank a $500,000 check and we purchased the $2.2 million dollar building. The $500,000 came from monies that our church had saved for several years and multiple miracle provisions from Mike and hundreds of others who sacrificed to be part of this miracle. Today that racquetball club is home of Harvest Community Church that serves about eight hundred people living on the south side of Milwaukee.

I've seen this kind of provision over and over and have thus been encouraged to step out in faith. At my current church, the church changed my role from being the senior pastor to becoming a full-time generosity minister to Christians and churches across the country and around the world. In this new global role my salary from the church is $1 per year plus medical benefits. Someone told me that in Texas, they would call my title, position, and pay, "big hat and no cattle." For a lot of people that would be sheer insanity, but for those of us acquainted with the ways of our powerful and active God, it makes perfect sense. "Unending riches, honor, justice, and righteousness are mine to distribute," He assures us in Proverbs 8:18 (TLB). "My gifts are better than the purest gold or sterling silver. . . . Those who love and follow me are indeed wealthy. I fill their treasuries" (vss. 19–21 TLB). While we have no guaranteed salary coming in every week, God now provides for my family and my ministry through speaking engagements, book and CD sales, creative provisions, and unexpected donations that come to us.

I was teaching a seminar at a conference once and mentioned that I was going on a ministry trip to India. Afterward, a man approached me and offered to buy me lunch. Over lunch he asked me when I was going to India. "I'm going in two weeks," I answered.

"How are you going to pay for it?"

"I don't know; I haven't figured it out yet."

"I'd like to help you. Does your church have a stock brokerage account?"

I said yes and gave him my assistant's phone number, but I didn't think to write down his name or number. I thought maybe he was going to send me a few hundred dollars, which would have been helpful for this trip. On Monday my secretary called and said that some unknown person had put $4,000 worth of stock into our brokerage account for my ministry trip to India. We sold the stock and I went to India. The cost of everything involved with this specific ministry trip? You guessed it: $4,000. God filled my treasury to meet a specific need.

So we have seen how God can provide through a main income, through extra income, and through unexpected provision. The question is not, "Will God provide?" but "Will we live lives that glorify our Provider? Will we seek to meet the needs of others? Will we look to God as our Provider?"

TRUE WEALTH AND CONTENTMENT

Be aware, however, that understanding that God is our Provider is not the same as the "prosperity gospel," a common heresy that says that God will bless us materially—in fact, is nearly obligated to do so—if we will just have enough faith. The prosperity gospel is all about *getting*, not *giving*. It's all about more for *us* instead of more for *God*. It's all about us instead of being all about Him. Yes, the God who provides for us often sends us resources to meet our needs, and often our desires, but He is not interested in meeting our *greeds*! And oftentimes He gives us things that are far more valuable than money. He provides wisdom, peace, strength, guidance, joy, contentment, and so much more! There are many people who are very wealthy financially who do not have these things. On the other hand, during a ministry trip to India, my wife, Sandi, asked a fellow believer if it was true that many of the country's Christians were very poor. "Yes," her friend countered with a twinkle in his eye, "but we are rich in Christ!" This man had true riches and godly contentment.

> *The question is not "Will God provide?" but "Will we live lives that glorify our Provider?"*

One of the most contented, joyful, and grateful couples I ever met lived in an old and run down 15' x 20' rental house in Arizona. Some of us have homes with rooms bigger than that. They and their eight-year-old, paralyzed, wheelchair-bound son lived in those three hundred square feet and they made about $800 a month. When I walked into that little home, there was joy radiating from within. This family had next to nothing in this world's possessions, but I've never been in a more joyful house, and never seen such contentment and gratefulness. God was their Provider, and they rejoiced at how He was meeting their needs and giving their family so much love, joy, and contentment.

"Godliness with contentment is great gain," Paul told Timothy. "For we brought nothing into the world, and we can take nothing out of it. But if we have food and clothing, we will be content with that" (1 Timothy 6:6–8).

Many of today's economic problems are, at root, symptoms of our society's pervasive love of money. People wanted to have bigger cars and houses than they could afford, and there were always accommodating brokers and loan officers to help them. The financial carnage we have witnessed should be no surprise. As Paul said, "Some people, eager for money, have wandered from the faith and pierced themselves with many griefs" (1 Timothy 6:10). Living our lives to pursue money and the things that money can buy will bring h, finances, and our families.

:d with a very wealthy man to invite him to help to a ministry I was involved with at the time. He iving me a tour of his home and all of his expen- hat he had gathered from his travels around the .. .. I was leaving he told me he was not able to help the ministry. As I was walking out the front door, there was a dirty young man who had obviously lived a life doing drugs who was doing yard work around his bushes. The young man looked up at me from where he was kneeling in the dirt and the wealthy man said, "That's my son," and he walked me to my car to say good-bye. I felt sorry for the man. He thought he was rich. He had everything that money could buy—fancy cars, big home, expensive possessions, luxury trips, and more. And yet as I drove away I realized how poor he really was. He was miserly, tight-fisted, had a troubled family and an anemic faith.

But how do you and I stay free from the love of money that will hurt our faith and our family? Ecclesiastes 5:10 provides a fail-safe heart check: "Whoever loves money never has money enough; whoever loves wealth is never satisfied with his income." In other words, we know we love our money if we're not grateful, content, or thankful. We don't see money as God's provision, and we never have enough of it. If this truth touches close to home, examine your heart. How? By seeing who is sitting on its throne: King Mammon or the Lord Jesus. As Jesus said, we can only serve one master (Matthew 6:24). God does not want you to pursue money; He wants you to pursue Him. In pursuing Him and living for His glory, you will bless others and experience God's provisions.

PROVISION AND WISE STEWARDSHIP

Let's talk about some other ways God provides for us. Some-times it's through our work or extra income, or perhaps via a totally unexpected provision that displays His power with glorious clarity. Other times God provides more subtly, less dramatically. God should also get the credit when we diligently work and use our minds to get a good deal on something. As with most things in life, it's important to do a little research.

Recently I took my vehicle to a mechanic and received a list of repairs that was going to cost hundreds of dollars. I asked the mechanic to do just a couple of things that I knew needed to be done. I wondered whether there might be some laid-off or experienced freelance mechanics on Craigslist.com (a website that offers free local advertising) who would be happy to work on my vehicle for a more affordable price than what the shop was going to cost me at $100 per hour for labor. So I found and e-mailed five mechanics and asked for bids on the remaining work, which the original mechanic had said would come to about $500. I chose someone who had been a mechanic for twenty years, and he was willing to come right to my house and do all the work on my car. When he went over the list with me and checked out my car, he said, "They're kind of making some of this up." I'm not mechanically minded so I had no idea. When everything that needed to be done was completed, the bill was only $200 instead of the $500 the shop was going to charge me. I don't know about you, but for me it was like someone handed me $300 in cash. I believe this was part of God's provision for my family. Three hundred dollars not spent on a vehicle meant it could be used for something else.

If cash is tight, you have to start thinking this way, and it is good stewardship in any case. Using your brain doesn't mean you're suddenly trusting God less; it just means you're trusting Him in a new way. Proverbs 24:5 says, "A man of knowledge increases strength." Whether the money comes through an unexpected provision or through some wise research and decisions on your part, you still have to see your needs as being met by God.

Recently, we decided to get a new vacuum cleaner. We checked

Craigslist.com and found the exact vacuum cleaner (a store demo) for $250 cheaper than we could have bought it at a store. Again, in our family, we see all of these things as part of God's provisions.

Other times we receive God's provision through His people's help and hospitality. Recently, I took my family on a vacation to California. A friend gave us a free place to stay for four nights and got us free tickets to Disneyland. Her hospitality saved our family hundreds of dollars.

In my vocation as a global generosity minister I often travel around the country and sometimes overseas. You might be surprised by how little I spend on food and lodging. How does this happen? Frequently I am invited to stay with fellow Christians. Whenever I'm in Atlanta, my good friend Jerry Schriver with the Christian Stewardship Network lets me stay in his spare guest room. Jerry and Pat's generosity can save me hundreds of dollars over the conference hotel. I also have good friends in Milwaukee, in Minneapolis, and elsewhere who have given me and my family an open invitation to stay in their homes when we are coming through town. When someone gives you a place to stay and you don't have to spend that money on a hotel, it's the same as if someone handed you $100, $200, or more. It's God's blessing to you through His people. The Bible says that every good and perfect gift comes down from the Father of Lights (James 1:17), and so He's the one who gets the ultimate credit. But there's no denying the fact that His children are often His channels of blessing.

In the same way, our family has provided food and lodging for many people over the years. Sometimes it has been for one meal or lodging for a night, but other times we have had people stay with us for days, weeks, months, and even years! We have taken in an unwed mother, singles and families struggling with debt issues, single young women, internationals, exchange students, and more. We even had three sisters from Latin America who individually came to live with our family after they graduated from high school.

Lisa stayed with us for two years, Leana stayed with us for six years, and Elena stayed with us for one year. These three young women and now their husbands have become like family to us.

It works both ways, of course. Just as we must always be ready to receive help from God's people, so we should be prepared to give it. Romans 12:13 reminds us, "When God's children are in need, you be the one to help them out. And get into the habit of inviting guests home for dinner or, if they need lodging, for the night" (TLB). In other words, if you have a spare car and someone needs it, loan it—or give it. Maybe you know someone who needs babysitting, or a meal, or a car or house repair, and you have the skills and resources to help. Come alongside that person and lend a hand.

The twenty-first-century church has fallen out of the habit of providing help to its members, much less to the wider society. With all of our smart phones, iPods, and technology, we seem to have forgotten how to roll up our sleeves and get involved. We think someone else will do it, but the Lord is calling us to do it.

We need to learn to be Jesus with skin on. We need to be the answer to someone's need and prayer. Not only should we learn to receive from God, but we also need to learn how to be God's agent of blessing for someone else. When you see a need and step up to meet it—whether it's by your time, efforts, resources, or whatever—it's a wonderful opportunity to "let your light shine before men, that they may see your good deeds and praise your Father in heaven" (Matthew 5:16). We have found that at Thanksgiving, many international people are left all alone from their job or schooling as all of America takes four days off. Over the years, we have found this is a wonderful time to invite foreign guests into our home for a meal. In recent years we have had people from Puerto Rico, Australia, El Salvador, Germany, Israel, India, Colombia, Iraq, England, and other places in our home so they wouldn't have to sit alone in their rooms or homes while others were enjoying family and friends.

> *Not only should we learn to receive from God, but we also need to learn how to be God's agent of blessing for someone else.*

A colleague of mine lost his job during the recession. His wife had been staying home with their three young children, and they didn't know how they were going to pay their bills, which, as with most of us, were many. As this couple tried to get their bearings, their church, other Christians, and friends in the community sprang into action. One came over and fixed their ailing computer. A neighbor across the street offered to pick up low-cost groceries at their church. Then the checks and cash gifts started arriving: this one for $20, that one for $100, another for $500—and many of them came anonymously. An older couple started bringing over jars of homemade strawberry-rhubarb jam. The daughter's music teacher waived the $35 registration fee for summer orchestra; the college student who mowed their lawn every week started doing it for free.

This couple, not surprisingly, saw these various gifts, large and small, as tangible expressions of God's love and provision. Soon the wife landed a full-time job (which they also saw as a divine gift) and the husband began receiving a steady stream of freelance work, and their situation greatly improved.

God can and will use you in this world to bring kindness, hospitality, and help to someone in need. When you see a need and sense God's call, don't wait to see if someone else will respond. You step in and meet the need. That's part of our call, our mandate. And being a channel for God's blessings is not a burden—or shouldn't be. It's a blessing. Remember, it is more blessed to give than to receive. God wants to use us in incredible ways and will do so if we make ourselves available.

Galatians 6:10 reminds us, "As we have opportunity, let us do good to all people." Whether it be a neighbor, a friend, a coworker, a person on the street, a stranger, or someone in the church family, we are to do good to that person. Then Paul continues, "especially to those who belong to the family of believers." Here the call focuses in particular on helping fellow believers. We have a special responsibility to assist, to bless other Christians.

A number of years ago my wife and I traveled and ministered in India for six weeks. During this season in our lives, we did not own or use any credit or debit cards. We just used cash, so we carefully budgeted and spent what we had to last for the six-week duration of the trip. At the end of our time in India, we headed with thankful hearts for the airport, our wallet nearly empty. Once we got there, however, the authorities told us that there was a problem with the plane we were about to board, and there wouldn't be another one for three days. We only had enough money for a single night's stay at a hotel. My wife, Sandi, asked, sensibly, "What are we going to do?" I said, "I have no idea, but let's pray."

It was Saturday night, so we found a hotel in Delhi and hoped to locate a church service for the next morning. We had heard of a church called Delhi Bible Fellowship and prayed that we could somehow find it in the city of twenty million people. So we looked it up in the hotel phone book. Imagine our complete surprise when we found out where Delhi Bible Fellowship was meeting. It was meeting in that hotel! In a city of millions, all we had to do was take the elevator to go to church!

So the next morning, our pockets empty of money but our hearts filled with gratitude to God, we entered the church service, a multinational gathering. During the time of greeting, someone asked us, "What are you doing here?"

"We've been here on a missions trip," I replied, "and we're staying in India for three extra days because our flight was cancelled."

"Where are you staying?"

"I don't know. I know where we stayed last night, but I don't know where we're staying the next few nights."

"What do you mean?"

"We don't have a credit card, and we are out of money after six weeks of traveling in India."

Then a Canadian couple worshiping there said, "Then you come home with us." This Canadian couple took us home. That night they slept on the couch while we slept in their bed. We were total strangers but they took us in. God provided. This couple was Jesus with skin on. And they did even more. Not only did they give us a place to stay, they paid for us to go down to Agra to see the Taj Mahal. "You can't come to India," they insisted, "without seeing the Taj Mahal!" And who were we to argue, when all this was so evidently God's provision? Who were we to proudly turn down their help and deny them God's blessing for blessing us? This episode, you see, was not only a God thing for us. It was also a God thing for these dear people. We were all aware that God was providing and blessing.

Our loving Provider is powerful and active, even today. He stands ready to help us, here and around the world, in ways that seem ordinary and in ways that are clearly extraordinary. As He does so, we are called to be grateful givers and grateful receivers of that help. The question is, are we ready to step outside our secular box and trust Him as our Provider?

***

For groups, classes, or family discussions, choose the most interesting three to five questions to discuss together.

1. Share a story about a time when someone's help or hospitality met a need in your life.

2. Who is someone you know right now in your church, work-place, or community that is a single parent, widow, fatherless child, foreigner, or military family? What could you or your group do for them to be "Jesus with skin on"?

3. What are some possessions or abilities you have that you could share with others and be a tremendous blessing to them? Examples might include recreational equipment, spare guest room, extra vehicle, social events, hobbies, special skills, etc.

4. If you received a bonus, overtime, unexpected cash, or an inheritance in the next several months, what ministry, missionary, needy person, or special project would you like to help with some of this money?

5. Share a story of a time when God provided cash or a needed item for you in a totally unexpected way.

Chapter 3

YOUR
RESOURCES

Let's step back for a moment. We have just reviewed how God provides income for us in ordinary, and sometimes extraordinary, ways. These resources come down to us, as it were, like manna from heaven. We are fed, directly or indirectly, by God's hand. But I wonder whether we sometimes fail to see how God has in many cases already provided for us. I have a plaque that says, "God feeds the birds of the air, but He doesn't throw the worms in the nest." God's provision is not merely a case of us looking to the future and waiting for Him to act. Often it is a matter of opening our eyes to how He has already acted for us, sometimes without our knowledge or request.

STORED-UP RESOURCES

I'm speaking of our stored-up resources. Some of us have more of these resources than others, but most of us in America and other Western countries have access to at least some of them, though we don't always recognize them as God's provision. These are things such as investments, insurance, pensions, equity in a home or property, savings, rentals, and other assets.

Yet, many people lack these stored-up resources, because in most cases they come only to those with the foresight to plan for them. Over half of the American people live paycheck to paycheck. Many of us don't think we can plan our lives more than a week ahead and are just happy if we can put food on the table and pay our bills.

But Proverbs 21:20 notes, "The wise man saves for the future" (TLB). The verb "saves" can also mean "prepares." A wise person, in other words, prepares for both the positives and the negatives of life—and most of us will face plenty of both. In the context of this book, the wise person makes financial plans for what is ahead: college, retirement, vacations, a car breakdown, an illness, a death, or whatever. Again, we are returning to the theme of using the mind that God gave us, which, after all, is one of the greatest provisions from God's hand. In fact, the word *capital* in *capitalism* is derived from the Latin word *caput*, which means "head." One could argue that God's greatest provision for us is our head. God wants us to use our minds, but not to totally rely on our own understanding. As pointed out earlier, Proverbs 3:5 says, "Trust in the Lord with all your heart and lean not on your own understanding."

But when we go back to Proverbs 21:20, the idea of saving for the future is only the first half of the verse. The rest of the verse warns us, "the foolish man spends whatever he gets." In other words, the fool spends all he or she receives, with nothing left over for the future. For the nearly half of the world's population that tries to survive on less than $2 a day, such a live-for-the-moment mentality is somewhat understandable. But even with the tens of thousands of dollars many of us make every year, according to the Bible, we have become a nation of fools, spending not just what we get but more than we get. For many people, instead of setting something aside for a rainy day, we consume all we get, and complain when the unexpected occurs—as it inevitably does. Cars do need to be repaired, children do need to go to the dentist, Christmas does occur every year, taxes must be paid, and insurance premiums do become due.

> *A wise person prepares for both the positives and the negatives of life—and most of us will face plenty of both.*

America is filled with foolish—yes, foolish—people who spend whatever they get and more. Many people somehow think that paying a $15 minimum payment on a $3,300 credit card bill is the way to live. The wise person, however, says, "No, I've got a plan. I'm preparing. I'm living below my means. I am moving toward the future with my eyes open to the realities of what is coming my way this month, this quarter, this year, and down the road."

In my own life the common wisdom was, "Just keep putting a regular portion of your salary into savings or investments, and someday it'll become a big mountain of money, down which will flow a river of gold." Well, the predictions of financial professionals fell flat and the ups and downs of a debt-ridden economy wreak havoc on people's homes, investments, and pensions.

For quite a while I was putting away hundreds every month, trying to follow the advice of the financial planners on how to build my own mountain and hoping to send my children to college and plan for my retirement. There was just one problem: It never worked. My mountain never grew, whether due to the movements of the markets or other factors that I still don't totally understand to this day. Many people have their own stories that don't quite fit the textbook accounts of the riches that will be created through disciplined investing and diversification. It's not that the advice I heard was wrong; it's just that life is often more complicated than we have sometimes been led to believe. There are no financial guarantees in this world, as more and more of us are starting to realize. Rather than simply getting "a piece of the rock," we need to take our stand on the Rock.

My setting aside hundreds of dollars a month was getting us nowhere, and the dream of helping get my kids a college education seemed as distant as ever. A couple of years ago I finally admitted, "God, this isn't working. I'm trying to prepare for the future; I'm thinking of my kids and their college education and possible retirement years, but I feel like I am losing ground instead of gaining ground."

I received an answer, but it wasn't the one I expected. "You do need to prepare for the future," God quietly spoke to my heart, "but you're doing it the wrong way." I was relying on the magic of compound interest and the graphs financial professionals showed me, but He was telling me to rely on Him.

For me, this meant finding a unique ministry that would bring value to others—and income to our family. My wife, Sandi, and I turned in the standard playbook and took some of the money I had received as an inheritance and we developed and printed a devotional booklet called the *40 Day Spiritual Journey to a More Generous Life*. The reason we had to use some of our own money for this endeavor was that seven publishers turned down our book idea because they said that no one would ever want to buy a Bible devotional on living generously. So, we launched out on our own with some inheritance money we were going to put into the stock market and instead invested this money in the kingdom of God to serve God and bless others. In the last four years, we have had to print 500,000 copies to keep up with the demand! Hundreds and hun-

dreds of churches have ordered copies to give to every f.
ignite people's faith in God to provide, inspire greater gen
and increase giving. People from around the world have re<
permission to translate and print copies in over fifty lang
Because we have continued to maintain the lifestyle level of a
church pastor, most of the money we've received has been rein-
vested in God's work in our ministry, community, country, and
around the world. And eventually, a portion of this money will help
us meet some of our longer-term goals of helping our children with
their education and preparation for adulthood.

Following God's leading and investing in the kingdom of God
certainly has been a lot more exciting and meaningful than putting money in the stock market and daily checking the stock figures
and fretting about stock prices. Our retirement and education
monies are like the little boy's five loaves and two fishes. The Lord
Jesus took what we offered and He multiplied it to spiritually feed
thousands and to raise and release millions of dollars for God's
work around the world as the people who read the devotional
become more faithful and generous givers.

But I also realize that God leads many people to carefully save,
invest wisely, and take advantage of company pension funds or
IRAs to provide for future needs. A number of my friends and
family have wisely stored up for the future using time-tested
wealth-building strategies that are available to anyone who chooses
to use them. Does God provide for His children and His servants?
He has done so for us, and He will do it for you too, though no two
instances of His provision will look exactly alike.

To get started, ask yourself the following questions: "What am
I doing to prepare for the future? What do I have within me? What
do I have around me? What are my God-given resources, skills,
and abilities? What can I do to honor God and serve others in such
a way that God can use it to also help me meet some of my financial needs, both today and tomorrow?"

> *Give first to God, and then learn to look to Him to creatively and faithfully meet your needs from His unlimited resources.*

The Bible says that a wise person prepares for the future. It doesn't say a wealthy person. You don't have to have to be wealthy to prepare for the future, you only have to be wise. My friend Ron Blue, a financial author and advisor, was speaking at a conference I had organized. Ron has been an advisor to many people who are worth millions of dollars. I will never forget a point in his message when he said that many people ask him, "What is the secret to long-term financial success and stability?" You could have heard a pin drop in the conference room when he paused before giving his answer. Everyone in the room was listening attentively as he said, "The secret to long-term financial success and stability is spend less than you earn for a long, long time." That's it? Yup, that's it! The only thing I would add is, "Give to God first, and spend less than you earn for a long, long time." It doesn't do any good to have financial stability and success and not be generous regarding the things of God. Give first to God, and then learn to look to Him to creatively and faithfully meet your needs from His unlimited resources.

I heard of one pastor who never made more than $20,000 in a year, but he slowly bought up rental properties over the course of his ministry life. He lived in one, but rented out the others so that he was always able to be generous to God's work while having enough income to live on. This pastor, despite what many would consider to be a modest income, was prepared for the future. He didn't make excuses, he just began to use what he had to prepare for the future.

Another pastor who is a friend of mine told me that his grandson was graduating from high school and he and some of his friends wanted to go on an around-the-world missions trip but didn't know how they would raise the money. One day while working on his computer he was thinking, "I wish I could help my grandson go on this missions trip," but he didn't have any extra money. Suddenly, he noticed that a penny stock he had bought years before for 60¢ a share had jumped to over $3, and immediately he clicked "sell." The trade brought in $13,000. My friend said, "I didn't need that money for myself. All of our real needs are met. So, I took that money and just poured it into the missions trip for my grandson and his friends!" He'd had those shares for years and then suddenly, in a moment, God opened the way and my friend opened his hand. As 1 Chronicles 29:12 says, "Wealth and honor come from you; you are the ruler of all things."

As we consider what other resources we have at our disposal, we don't have to venture far from home. In fact, let's zero in on the wealth available within the four walls of our dwellings. Psalm 112:1–3 starts out, "Blessed is the man who fears the Lord, who finds great delight in his commands. His children will be mighty in the land." The foundation of God's provision is a right relationship with Him. We cannot expect God to be our Provider if we avoid Him or disobey His commands. But if we trust Him, not only will He take care of our needs, He will bless our families. And this blessing touches both the material and the spiritual: "The generation of the upright will be blessed. Wealth and riches are in his house, and his righteousness endures forever." Again, we see here the idea of not just consuming wealth, but having it at our disposal for future needs. The righteous have access to resources within the home.

While I was growing up, my father was a fireman. Six weeks before he died he wrote down all the financial information my mother needed to know on a napkin. "When I die," he told her, "one of the things that will happen is the fire department will get in touch with you. I took out a special insurance policy for $125,000. You just need to be aware of that." Sure enough, a month or so after he died, the fire department sent her a letter detailing the existence of the insurance policy my dad told her about. With the letter was a check for $25,000. She was instructed to sign a release, indicating that she had been paid in full.

Surprised, my mother went back to her little napkin and saw that my dad had written down $125,000. She called me and said, "Brian, I think Dad made a mistake." I said, "Mom, I don't think Dad made a mistake. I think you need to call the fire department and tell them that your husband wrote down on a piece of paper that you were to get $125,000." So she called them. "We're sorry," came the reply. "We made a typographical error. Return the check and we'll send you $125,000." The moral here: Keep good financial records. Pass along important information to your spouse and loved ones. You are responsible to know what's in your accounts and the account numbers and to pass this information along to others who need to know. If you don't get that information written down, you'll lose resources that God had intended for you and your family. Someone once told me that more than 35 percent of insurance policies are never claimed, and no insurance company is ever going to call you and ask, "Did anybody die in your family recently?"

When my mother later passed away, I needed to sort through her things. She had all her finances in one place and also what looked like a junky pile of papers in another. Before responding to my natural urge to scoop up those papers and throw them away, I felt prompted to go through them.

After I got started in what I thought would be a quick task, suddenly I saw two little yellowed sheets. They were from 1956. My mother had taken out a company insurance policy when she had worked outside the home decades before. The premium was 10¢ a week, taken as a payroll deduction. Nobody in our family had ever heard about this policy.

I looked up the company on Google and found out it was still in existence. I called the number and asked, "Is this insurance policy still good?" and a company representative replied, "Absolutely. They're paid in full and they're worth thousands of dollars." In my late mother's house was an apparently worthless pile of papers that concealed something of real worth. Such unexpected wealth and riches, there all along, were part of God's provisions in our life.

After these personal experiences and also sitting as a pastor with many spouses and families who lost loved ones, I discovered that most spouses and families have very little information about finances, family history, funeral wishes, and more. This led me to write a fifty-two-page manual of helpful forms called the *Because I Love You Family Organizer*. Thousands of copies of this manual have been distributed by churches, financial professionals, ministries, medical groups, and others to help people get their lives and houses in order for themselves, their spouses, and their families. In addition to this manual, families can go to websites like www.missingmoney.com to find out if there are any unclaimed assets or monies from old insurance accounts, bank accounts, etc.

All of these provisions can be part of the way God may choose to provide.

But we have to remember that while we may participate in years of accumulating, God calls us at times to distribute our wealth and riches. "Freely you have received," Jesus said, "freely give" (Matthew 10:8). Yes, you may accumulate for a season of life, but there are times throughout your life and near the end of your life when God will say, "Open your hand. Let it go. Release it."

This happened in King David's life. After years of winning battles, taking plunder, and collecting tributes, David said in 1 Chronicles 29:2–3, "With all my resources I have provided for the temple of my God. . . . Besides, in my devotion to the temple of my God I now give my personal treasures of gold and silver for the temple of my God, over and above everything I have provided for this holy temple." David saw honoring the Lord with his wealth to be more important than building his own financial mountain. We should do the same.

As you go through various seasons of life, you will accumulate things. But as you move beyond each season, what are you going to do with all the things you've accumulated? Baby years will pass and your children will become older. Teen years will pass and your teens will become adults and move away. The need for a big house will decrease as your children have their own families. In each season we tend to intentionally accumulate. But if we're children of God, we need to also learn to intentionally de-clutter and de-accumulate. Pass these items along to others who could use them or for ministry purposes in the kingdom of God. Or sell the items and pass along the proceeds. Have you recently passed through a season of accumulating things and now you find you no longer need them and aren't using them? Ask the Lord what you should do with what you have.

Again, this takes planning and effort. For those in their sixties and beyond, I have discovered that if you're working with a good planned-giving professional, you can save on your taxes and use some of your money and assets to help expand the kingdom of God. Your children will receive exactly what they would have, but instead of giving Uncle Sam a huge chunk of your assets, you can give it to the kingdom of God. In our later seasons of life, it's very important to talk with someone who really understands how to handle your accumulated assets and estate plans for maximum ministry impact. A friend of mine had an estate worth $5 million. His children were going to get $2 million and the government was going to get $3 million. But by working with a Christian estate-planning professional, he was able to still give his children $2 million, the government got half a million, and God's kingdom work got $2.5 million!

Regarding providing for our heirs, Proverbs 13:22 says, "A good man leaves an inheritance for his children's children, but a sinner's wealth is stored up for the righteous." Too often seniors are expected to spend all of their wealth on themselves—on vacations, toys, and trinkets. This verse, however, says we are to think of others. Are you preparing to help not just yourself but also your children—and even your children's children? And this help should come not just in the financial realm, which is important enough, but in the spiritual realm. Ask yourself: "What will my spiritual legacy be?"

Several times when Sandi and I were in our twenties, thirties, and forties, our parents gave us some early inheritance monies. Once they helped us when we adopted our daughter, Bethany, from India. Another time my parents helped me get started in a business. When we moved into one of our homes, my mother gave us money to help buy furnishings. A wise person once said, "Do yer' givin' while yer' livin' so you'll be a knowin' where it's a goin'." In America today you can give $12,000 to any person you want, tax-free. An early inheritance can be a great blessing. One couple paid for Christian schooling for all of their grandchildren. Another set of grandparents gave their grandchildren the choice to attend one of two Christian universities. They had seventeen grandchildren, and most of us understand that Christian schooling is not cheap. But when they got through the seventeen grandchildren, this generous couple still had some money left, so they started paying for friends of the family to get a Christian college education. Their vision was that their resources would bless future generations— and they have.

EXTERNAL RESOURCES

Now we come to resources outside of our home. These outside resources are controlled by others but ultimately are owned by God our Provider—and are His to distribute as He sees fit for the furtherance of His own glory.

We see this in Nehemiah 2:4–5. Nehemiah, living in exile, is the trusted servant of King Artaxerxes. He has a burden for Jerusalem and has been praying, fasting, and weeping. Hundreds of miles

> *Are you preparing to help not just yourself but also your children—and even your children's children? Ask yourself: "What will my spiritual legacy be?"*

from the holy city in Babylon, the king notices his servant's distress and asks, "What do you want?" How many of us have ever had a wealthy person ask what we want? How should we answer them? Before Nehemiah replied, he did something important. "Then I prayed to the God of heaven," he writes. It's an arrow of prayer. The king is right here, Nehemiah is right here, and God is right here. The king says, "What do you want?" and Nehemiah prays straight to the throne of heaven. "God, help me now," he may have thought. "I'm going to open my mouth in one second. Fill it with what You want me to say."

So Nehemiah reports, "I answered the king, 'If it pleases the king and if your servant has found favor in his sight, let him send me to the city in Judah where my fathers are buried so that I can rebuild it.'" A bold request and a good one. Nehemiah is requesting a ticket back. Then he goes on to say, "And, by the way, we need some lumber. And, by the way, we need this and we need that." The king says, "No problem," and he authorizes a government grant, not for his own kingdom, but for the kingdom of God, for the advancement of God's work in that generation. Artaxerxes is like a major donor, and he says, "Yes, I'm glad to do that."

As this episode shows, God can use a major donor—including a nonbelieving government—to supply the needs of God's servant. Uncle Sam sometimes helps with our education. The GI Bill helped thousands. Recently I had lunch with a young married man in seminary. After six years of serving with the Air Force, the government helped him get his undergraduate degree and was now helping to pay his way through seminary. He told me the story that he had quit his job to go to seminary because he and his wife believed that this was what God wanted him to do, even though they didn't have any guaranteed income and had four young children at home. It turns out that after he resigned his position and signed up for seminary that he found out that the government would help cover his housing costs while he was in school full-time. He was told to go to a specific website and put his zip code into one of the computer forms and it would calculate the value of his housing allowance. When he put in his zip code, the number that popped up was the exact amount he paid monthly for his house. He had quit his job and signed up for seminary *not* knowing how God was going to provide, and then he and his wife were blown away when their tuition was paid for and the housing allowance he received covered his exact housing costs! In God's grace, providence, and sovereignty, He uses the government to help accomplish His good purposes.

Another outside source of God's provision, as we have already seen, is a local church congregation. Galatians 5:13 reminds us, "Serve one another in love." I am so grateful for the church where I serve. When I arrived, the congregation gave $6,000 to $7,000 per year to help people with financial needs—a significant but still quite modest amount. As our church has grown in our understanding of God as our Provider, we have multiplied our giving. Our benevolence ministry recently distributed about $60,000, helping over two hundred families with utilities, medical challenges, mortgages or rent, and money for gas, food, and other needs. The church can meet needs in ways individuals and governments cannot—both financial and spiritual. Houses of worship are a powerful agent for good in a hurting society, particularly when they understand God as Provider.

And God sometimes provides in miraculous ways. Of course, He provides through the other ways highlighted in this book, and that is fine. Everything belongs to Him, and He is sovereign. Other times, however, He works something so amazing and direct that His miraculous fingerprint is unmistakable. We can't predict when this will happen and certainly can't demand it, but the Lord our Provider is free to provide however He wants.

Earlier we mentioned the story of the little boy with the five loaves and two fish (John 6:5–11). The boy gave what he had to Jesus, and Jesus multiplied it. The woman poured out perfume on Jesus' feet that was worth a year's wages (Mark 14:3–9)! You will discover that if you give whatever you have to Jesus—whether it's little or much—He can take it, multiply it, and do something special and even miraculous with it.

John Bechtel, a missionary in Hong Kong, felt called to start a Christian camp. Hong Kong, of course, is a small place and land there is extremely costly. John found a multimillion-dollar property that was for sale that he could buy at a discounted price if he could come up with the money. As a missionary, he didn't have any money, so the owners gave him time to raise it from among his overseas connections.

After some months of trying to raise the money, nobody gave any generous gifts to make the purchase possible. Then John received a letter from a young girl with $1 enclosed to help him buy the camp to reach children in Hong Kong for Jesus. John took the letter and $1 to the sellers and they decided to accept the $1 as payment in full for their property and all of its buildings. Wow! Talk about God's provisions. God took a little girl's gift and miraculously multiplied it for His glory and purposes.

The property became Suen Dough Christian camp, and my wife and I visited the camp on a ministry trip to Asia. Over a million people have attended this camp in the last two decades, and over one hundred thousand have come to Christ because of the investment of a girl who gave what she had. She shared it, Jesus took it, and He multiplied it.

A very dear friend shared with me another amazing story of God's provisions from external resources. About twenty years ago my friend was a tool machinist and made just over $30,000 per year. His wife stayed home and homeschooled the kids. So you can imagine that this couple didn't have a lot of extra cash lying around. Yet, they were faithful givers to the Lord out of the little that they had and had even started an outreach ministry based on the principle that "God would provide what they needed as they needed it." After they heard me teach on finances and generosity at a camp, they felt a desire from the Lord to pay off their mortgage early so they could be completely debt-free. So they began to pray about it and started paying a little extra money toward the principal.

One night in the middle of winter they heard a knock and opened the door. It was snowing outside and no one was there. They looked down and found an envelope taped to the door with their name on it. A little confused, they closed the door and their young son said he saw a shadowy figure running into the forested area away from their house. When they opened the envelope they discovered that it was filled with money, and a 3 x 5 card inside said, "Acts 4:32: 'All the believers were one in heart and mind. No one claimed that any of his possessions was his own, but they shared everything they had.' We are family. PTL!" When they counted the money, it was the amount they owed on their home within a few dollars.

Now I know this is a very unusual story. And if I didn't know the couple personally, I would probably doubt that it ever happened. But this story is always a wonderful reminder to me about God's incredible creativity and grace in how He can choose to provide. I wouldn't advise you to keep looking on your front porch for a bag of money to appear. The truth is, this couple wasn't looking for a bag of money on their porch, but in God's sovereignty He led someone to place it there with the exact amount of money they needed to become debt free after they had been diligently working on paying off their mortgage early.

Though this couple's story is unusual, such events are not unbiblical. In 2 Kings 4:1–7, one of the prophet Elisha's students dies, and his indebted family suddenly faces disaster. "The wife of a man from the company of the prophets cried out to Elisha, 'Your servant my husband is dead, and you know that he revered the Lord. But now his creditor is coming to take my two boys as his slaves.'"

Like Jesus before the miraculous feeding, Elisha asks what resources are already available. "Elisha replied to her, 'How can I help you? Tell me, what do you have in your house?'" It always starts with, "Tell me what you have." God will ask you, "What do you have? What skills? What abilities? What is in your hands? What is in your power? What is under your authority? Don't worry about anyone else; what do you have?" Like this woman, we are tempted to say, "Nothing." But look a little closer: "'Your servant has nothing there at all,' she said, 'except a little oil.'"

When God prepares you to do His work, He will always ask, "What do you have? What are you doing with it? Are you learning to be faithful with little so that you might someday be faithful with much?" Elisha replies, "Go around and ask all your neighbors for empty jars. Don't ask for just a few." In other words, start with what you have, however little it is. Then ask those around you, "Hey, could you help out here?" Go to family, friends, neighbors. Now you are prepared to see God provide. Elisha continues, "Then go inside and shut the door behind you and your sons. Pour oil into all the jars, and as each is filled, put it to one side."

In this case, the widow has participated in the miracle. If she hadn't faithfully followed Elisha's instructions, it is probably safe to assume that she wouldn't have received anything. But the glory still belongs to her heavenly Provider. "They brought the jars to her and she kept pouring. When all the jars were full, she said to her son, 'Bring me another one.' But he replied, 'There is not a jar left.' Then the oil stopped flowing. She went and told the man of God, and he said, 'Go, sell the oil and pay your debts. You and your sons can live on what is left.'"

One colleague lost his job in the recession, and his wife started looking for a position to pick up the financial slack. She was concerned because she had not been a part of the full-time workforce for years and might not have any marketable skills. Through God's miraculous provision, however, within weeks she was chosen over fifty other candidates and landed a job that provided much-needed resources for the family. Yet she was the one who updated her resume, researched the company, took the employment tests, and went on the interviews.

Many times God says to us, "I want you involved in the process. I'm going to provide for you and stretch your meager resources more than you ever dreamed possible, but you are going to have to work with Me." God always provides, but He does it in many ways. We need to be prepared to recognize and participate in His provisions. How we respond is the subject of the next chapter.

For groups, classes, or family discussions, choose the most interesting three to five questions to discuss together.

1. Many spouses do not know where information is on any life insurance or financial accounts. What steps do you think you'll need to take so that both of you have access to important financial information?
2. If you have a will, trust, or written estate plans, share what steps you went through to get this done. If you haven't done this yet, what are some things you need to do or decide to accomplish this?
3. If you have remembered the Lord's work in your estate plans, share why you felt it was important to do this and how you decided where the money should go.

4. If you have ever received any early inheritance monies or a generous financial gift from someone, how was the money utilized?

5. If or when you have children or grandchildren and you had the financial means to help, what is something you would like to help them with financially (examples might be a vehicle, education, starting a business, home, furniture/furnishings, etc.)?

6. What were your thoughts about the $1 gift that bought the camp in Hong Kong? How did this make you feel about the importance of your own generosity?

Chapter 4

YOUR
RESPONSE

These days many people are afraid of what has happened to our economy, and what might happen in the future. What at one time felt stable—housing prices, stock market, banks, mortgage companies, big car companies, pension funds—now feels shaky, unstable, and insecure. Things many people counted on for their financial security, like a good job, a home, and a 401(k), have collapsed like the proverbial house built on sand. Even those of us still getting by financially often dwell on the ugly possibilities: If my income goes away, what's going to happen to me? If my job disappears, where will I work? If my company goes south, can I find work in the same industry—or any work at all? If my marriage fails, what's going to happen to me?

Such fear, though understandable, is not God's plan for the Christian who is learning to experience God as Provider. We are now on an exciting journey of discovery. While others may fret and fear, we have the privilege of walking by faith and experiencing God in ways that show He is bigger than currencies, economies, job markets, paychecks, and investment plans. On this path we are not passive drones but active participants in God's divine plans to provide for us and care for us as we honor Him and seek to serve others. While all of His provisions are all pure grace, they invite a response of faith, and that faithful response in turn opens the door to more of God's blessings, whether spiritual or material. A steward's lifestyle is a virtuous cycle. When we prove we can be trusted with a little, we often receive even more to use for His kingdom. As Jesus said, if we are faithful with a few things, He will put us in charge of many things (Matthew 25:23).

> *When we prove we can be trusted with a little, we often receive even more to use for His kingdom.*

This chapter takes us a few steps further along this path, and our financial lives will necessarily look different than those of our neighbors. A lot of people live beyond their means, which is a key factor in some of the recent economic upheavals. A big problem in America today is that a lot of people have taken on obligations that literally put them behind a little bit more every single month. Some people stack their financial obligations one on top of another, and every month they take a run at this financial wall and can't vault over it. Those who live beyond their means not only can't get over the wall, they see it grow higher every month. If your wall is too big (and growing bigger), it won't help to put on a new pair of track shoes; you have to lower the wall, and keep it down.

But experiencing God as your Provider is not about merely

learning to live within your means. It's learning to first honor God with whatever He gives you, setting aside something for future needs, and learning to live below your means. For many people, this goal will require some important lifestyle changes that we can only accomplish with God's help, grace, and guidance.

ADJUSTING YOUR LIFESTYLE

To begin with, this means decreasing ongoing expenses and avoiding or eliminating indebtedness.

Proverbs 11:1 shows us how to get started. "The Lord abhors dishonest scales," it says, "but accurate weights are his delight." This verse extols honesty in business, but by application it also commends honesty in our family finances. In other words, our books need to balance. As much as we might wish we had more resources at our disposal, we cannot lie to ourselves about our budgets and resources.

Years ago I saw a political cartoon that showed how our government spends money. The cartoon showed the president saying that our economy was like a pie. One half of the pie was for domestic issues, another half of the pie was for foreign issues, and the third half of the pie was to run government operations. The problem is, the government doesn't have three halves of a pie and neither do we! I have also heard it said that when our outgo exceeds our income, our upkeep leads to our downfall! Eventually, being dishonest about our financial situation will lead to future crisis points in our lives—whether we're the government, a company, or a family.

If we're ever going to get on higher financial ground, we must get the facts, and face the facts, of where we are in our financial and faith journeys.

We also must learn to be careful about who we listen to when it comes to money decisions. Some mortgage brokers and real estate agents will tell you that you can afford more house than you really can. A car dealer will try to get you into the most expensive vehicle on the lot. The dealer really doesn't care whether you can afford it; that's your problem. His problem, though many dealers are honest and ethical, is figuring out how to get you to open your wallet and spend as much as possible. It's up to you to keep an eye on what is affordable. The desire for more and living beyond one's means always leads to trouble in the future.

Each of us has 100 percent of our resources to work with. With this 100 percent we need to honor God with our finances, pay our taxes, live our lives, and save and invest for the future. When my children were about four years old, we started each of them out with an envelope system. We gave them three envelopes and told them that money has three purposes: The first purpose is to give to God, the second purpose is to save for the future, and the third purpose is to spend for current needs. Whenever they got any money (birthdays, allowances, Christmas, work projects, etc.), we would take them into our bedroom and carefully divide the money into the three envelopes. When my oldest son turned sixteen, I told him there was now a fourth envelope we needed to add that was called taxes! The truth is that many people have not learned nor understood that whatever resources they have must be divided between these four categories and they spend all they have on the "current needs" envelope.

In this culture, if you're not honest with yourself about the four purposes of money, you'll commit too much money to house, to car, to entertainment or recreation, or to something else you are persuaded that you "need." But you won't be able to scale that wall. Admitting, "This isn't working," is humbling. In our natural pride and arrogance, we think, "This is my stuff, this is what I worked for, and this is what I want." But ultimately, if you can't balance your finances, you have dishonest scales.

In fact, the problem is worse than that. First Peter 5:5 warns,

"God opposes the proud." If you are overly proud about your stuff and your income, God will oppose you. So what can you do? Drop your pride and run to God. Yes, God opposes the proud, but the rest of the verse says, "but gives grace to the humble." He gives grace—unmerited favor—to the humble, those willing to say, "Lord, I can't do this. I need Your help." The next verse encourages us, "Humble yourselves, therefore, under God's mighty hand that he may lift you up in due time."

This lifting doesn't always happen overnight. Years ago, when I began to discover some of these principles, I owned a nicer car than I could afford. The payments, the gasoline, and the insurance were all beyond my means to pay and I had to humble myself. So I went from my shiny Chrysler Cordoba with payments to a little ugly brown Ford Pinto I bought for $800 in cash. I wanted to put a bumper sticker on my Pinto that said, "Don't laugh, it's paid for!" I would be out and see people driving expensive cars and I would think to myself that I would rather be driving a car that was paid for than driving a big fancy car with a sixty-month car payment that I couldn't afford.

I looked for other ways to save. Assessing my budget, I figured out that if I wanted to give to God and pay for all of life's necessities, then I could only afford $100 a month in rent. God graciously led me to live with seven Christian guys in a big house, and my monthly rent was the $100 I determined I could afford to pay. My time there was rich with spiritual growth and encouragement. God had provided again.

Once a young lady at our church in Milwaukee told me, "I want to give to God, but I need to eat, and I need a place to live. I can only do two of the three." I said, "Well, which ones do you want to do?"

"I want to give to God. I haven't been doing this, but I want to. And I probably better eat, so that means I can't afford my apartment."

I told her, "Then you need to trust God for a free place to live."

"Is that possible? Can I trust God for a free apartment?"

"Yes, let's pray for a free place to live."

A few weeks later, her prayer was answered: She moved in with us! Actually, she started living in a little apartment we had added onto our house that we made for visiting missionaries. The only thing was that no missionaries ever seemed to come to Milwaukee! So, instead of having a missionary apartment, we affectionately renamed it "the debtor's prison." We would allow individuals and even families who wanted to get out of debt and get their financial house in order to live there for free or at a minimal cost so they could begin to give to God, set aside some savings, and learn to adjust their lifestyle to live below their means. The debtor's prison apartment even came with the free use of a car we had purchased to share with people who lived there.

One of the couples who moved into our debtor's prison was a DINK. DINK means "double income, no kids." Because of medical reasons, our friends thought they weren't ever going to be able to have children, so on their double-income salary they bought one of the pricier houses in the neighborhood. They thought to themselves, "We can't have kids, so let's get a nice home." But God surprised them. They had one child. Then they had a second child. The wife wanted to be a stay-at-home mom, but they had a mortgage that required both of their salaries. So God gave them the grace to sell their beautiful home and move into our debtors' prison missionary apartment for six months until they could find a smaller home where they could raise their family on a mortgage that only required one salary. Eventually, this couple who thought they couldn't have any children were blessed by God with not just two children, but five.

An elderly friend at church was living on a fixed income. His son advised him to stop giving to the Lord so that my friend would have more money for himself. But instead, he decided he was willing to seek God for a more affordable place to live so he could continue to give generously to the Lord's work and to people in need. God provided in an amazing way and he moved into a high-rise complex in our city with a twelve-foot penthouse window view of Pikes Peak for $365 per month!

Some other friends of ours were financially burdened by living in a high-end luxury home in the suburbs that took 50 to 60 percent of their income and brought a lot of financial pressure into their lives. God gave them the grace to be able to sell their home, downsize their possessions, and move into a rental property in a working-class neighborhood. But God used this in their lives in amazing ways. Within several months of downsizing their home, the husband's company needed an executive to move to Paris, France, for a few years. He was given this promotion and a raise because he was ready to go immediately and wasn't shackled down by a house and possessions. His family moved to Paris at the expense of the company, and they also became actively involved in a church plant that reached many people for Christ.

If you're serious about living below your means, it makes sense to know what your means actually are. Do an audit of your stuff and look at all of your expenditures. Find out how much goes for groceries, for the house, for cars, vacations, gifts, insurance, entertainment, etc. Monitor every category of spending in your life and look for ways to do it better and more affordably. Ask yourself, "Is this really the best way to spend our money? Is this the way we want to be spending our money?" What you begin to save can go for giving, debt elimination, and other worthy things. It may be humbling at first, but God will give you His grace and He will lift you up.

Let's talk a little more about why we should avoid, reduce, and eliminate debt. Proverbs 22:7 states, "The rich rule over the poor, and the borrower is servant to the lender."

While it is not the "American way," you can learn to operate your life or business without taking on debt. This is entirely possible. Many Americans and businesses live far beyond their means, but just because "everyone's doing it" doesn't mean that *you* have to do it. God has a better plan for your life. Most people can be completely free from short-term indebtedness, including credit card debt, within one to three years just by being intentional. Within ten to twelve years, most people can have everything paid for, including our homes. The great news is that this can include you! The question is, Are we willing to humble ourselves to get there? Are we willing to become intentional to become debt free?

Now I'll admit that taking charge of our finances is not easy in our society. We are so dependent on others, so disconnected from the economic realities that those before us took for granted.

Many people, for example, don't even have a clear understanding of where our food comes from. I used to work at a Christian camp, and one of the staff members owned a small farm, so we would take the campers over to see the farm animals. One little girl returned from one of these visits very troubled, and the mother asked, "What happened over there?" She said, "Mommy, you wouldn't believe what they did to us over there." Her parents pressed for details: "Honey, what's wrong?"

"Well," came the pint-sized reply, "they had this goat, and they made the goat go to the bathroom in a bucket, and then they tried to make us drink it." She had no idea where milk comes from!

Instead of being clueless on how life and our finances work, we need to get clued in. We need to be alert to the many ways God can provide.

My friend Tom lived in a small town in northern Wisconsin. He was suffering from cancer and was extremely weak. It was the start of deer hunting season one fall, and Tom said to me, "Can you please pray for me?" I asked, "What do you need prayer for?" "I need to go get this winter's food. I've got to shoot a deer or we're not going to have meat this winter," he replied. How was Tom going to get the meat he and his family needed during deer hunting season when he was in a much-weakened condition? Deer are not easy to find, and are even more difficult to shoot, even when you are healthy. And it gets awfully cold in northern Wisconsin in the late fall. So I prayed for Tom, and together we asked God to provide. One day while Tom was driving, a deer was standing next to the road. Tom drives up and the deer doesn't move. In a weakened state, he gets out his shotgun, puts on his deer permit tag and orange vest, and the deer is still standing there. He leans up against the truck for support, and he shoots the deer on the side of the road! For anyone who has ever gone deer hunting, they understand the miracle of this story. We prayed for God to provide and He did. A lucky break? Hardly. God was Tom's Provider. God gave him the deer meat he needed. Of course, it helped immensely that Tom also knew how to handle a gun!"

Most people can be completely free from short-term indebtedness, including credit card debt, within one to three years just by being intentional.

Ecclesiastes 2:26 reminds us, "To the man who pleases him, God gives wisdom, knowledge and happiness, but to the sinner he gives the task of gathering and storing up wealth to hand it over to the one who pleases God."

God says, "If your life is focused on pleasing me, I'm going to help you, and I'm going to get the credit."

When my son Josh was sixteen he was unable to find a job. I told him that while there were no jobs to be had, there is always work to be done. I noticed that a number of widows in our church had graying cedar fences because of the hot Colorado sun. I helped set Josh up to begin to power wash and stain the widows' fences and also to make himself available to be hired to do other people's fences too. We were using Sandi's van to take his equipment and the stain to each job, and after a number of weeks she asked if we could get a different vehicle to haul all the equipment.

So, we began to pray for God's provision. I looked at our budget and felt that we could afford $2,000 to get Josh a truck for his growing little business. We quickly discovered that $2,000 doesn't get you much. The trucks we looked at were about twenty years old and usually in pretty poor shape. One afternoon at 4:30 I was perusing Craigslist. At about 4:20 someone had placed an ad for a used Chevy Tahoe SUV for $2,000 only about two miles from my house. I checked online for the typical price for this specific vehicle and the average selling price was $5,400. I called the guy and immediately went and over and looked at the truck. It was a beautiful vehicle and in great shape. Much better than we could ever have imagined. The guy said, "I need $2,000 tonight to pay some bills. If you give me $2,000 in cash, you can have it." I went to the bank, took $2,000 out of savings, handed him the money, and drove the truck away. Coincidence? No. It was God's provision in answer to our prayers and researching. Someone once told me that a "coincidence" is when something happens and God chooses to remain anonymous. This was not coincidence. God provided. The car keys were handed over to us as we sought to please God and serve people.

God's provisions are not always this simple and straightforward, however. Sometimes we go through very lean times—but the Lord is there in every case. So far I have faced two distinct times in my life when there was no work to be done, and no easy way to see where the provisions would come from. But God gave me a sense of calm and confidence.

He did it through 2 Kings 19:29–31, in which King Hezekiah is reassured of God's care and protection against the Assyrian invaders: "This will be the sign for you, O Hezekiah: This year you will eat what grows by itself." God would provide for the people, even though few crops were available. The second year for Judah would also be difficult: "and the second year what springs from that." Yet the hard times of scarcity would eventually be replaced by abundance. "But in the third year sow and reap, plant vineyards and eat their fruit. Once more a remnant . . . will take root below and bear fruit above. For out of Jerusalem will come a remnant, and out of Mount Zion a band of survivors."

I was on the board of a ministry that seemed on the verge of closing its doors. God encouraged me with this passage, saying, "I'm going to make this ministry and their staff a band of survivors. For two years, you're going to be cared for miraculously. In the third year you're going to have the strength and energy to thrive again." We all face seasons of life when we're down for the count, we don't have answers, and we don't know what to do. God says, "I'll be there. The day will come when you can begin again, but in this season of your life, you just have to let Me do it." And God kept this ministry going until things turned around. For two years they miraculously survived, and in the third year they began to thrive again.

I have experienced making $100 a month and I have even made over $50,000 a month. I wasn't any happier or more content on $50,000 than I was on $100.

Experiencing God as your Provider doesn't mean we get a deed to live on Easy Street. What it does mean is that He will faithfully supply our needs through thick and thin—and sometimes through a lot of thin. But in my own life's journey, I have discovered it is not how much you have, but how much of you God has! If He has all of you, then all of His can be at your disposal to fulfill His purposes in and through your life. In my adult life I have experienced making $100 a month and I have even made over $50,000 a month. I wasn't any happier or more content on $50,000 than I was on $100 a month. I have found that my contentment and my confidence come only from God, not what is in my checkbook.

DE-CLUTTERING

We can also experience His provision through observing the "less is more" principle. As Paul said, "I have learned the secret of being content in any and every situation, whether well fed or hungry, whether living in plenty or in want" (Philippians 4:12b). If God can give us stuff when we need it, perhaps we can give it away when we don't. In other words, sometimes it makes sense to share His plenty with others by de-cluttering our lives and de-accumulating our stuff. In fact, it has been my experience that we gain more contentment, satisfaction, and freedom by de-accumulating than by accumulating; by de-cluttering instead of adding more. Again, it is more blessed to give than to receive, and often the stuff we no longer need can bless someone else.

One elderly woman told me that when Christmas shopping for her adult children and grandchildren, she looks for gifts in her living room, on the shelves, and in the rest of the house. She identifies family knickknacks and heirlooms and carefully wraps them up and often tells the history and story behind each item. These special gifts, being de-accumulated near the end of her life, have become prized possessions of every family member.

Another elderly woman, eighty-eight, however, was visibly upset with me and this teaching on actively de-cluttering your life and de-accumulating things you no longer need. "I can't believe you are telling me to throw my perfectly good things away," she snapped. "I have beautiful and expensive baby furniture stored in my attic. I will never throw these things away." I reminded her of a young couple in our church with very little money just about to have their first baby. I told her she could bless them with this furniture. Finally, the light-bulb went on for her and she joyfully surprised this young couple with the gift of quality baby furniture they could never afford. God provided for this young couple items they needed and God provided grace and joy for this woman who learned to open her hands and bless others with what God had given her.

Many people could similarly bless others by going through their possessions, assets, and resources and selling them and giving some or all of the proceeds to God's work, or giving the actual items away to a family in need or ministry. Eventually, we must let go of everything we've ever possessed anyway. As I mentioned earlier, truly wise people do their "givin'" while they're livin'" so they are knowin' where it's goin'."

I'm going to start meddling for a moment. Think about every hook, nail, drawer, pile, shelf, cupboard, cabinet, closet, room, storage unit, shed, garage, home office, and building in your life. In each of these places, you probably have stuff you no longer need, use, or want. You're not going to use it, so why not get rid of it? Are you going to leave it there until you die and make it a loved one's problem someday? Step up to the plate and do the de-cluttering and de-accumulating now. You really can't take it with you. Paradoxically, not only will you feel a justifiable sense of relief when you clear out a lot of your stuff, but you will actually become more content and thankful for what you do keep. I recently heard that contentment is not gained by getting everything you want, but by being thankful for everything you have.

You can start small, working on just one of your cluttered areas. Not long ago, I de-cluttered my closet, removing two-thirds of my clothes that I seldom or never wear. Now I'm looking at the remaining third and feeling like I still have too much. I gave pants, suits, shirts, and ties to a ministry that was going to take clothing to Brazil. I heard recently that the pastor who received some of my suits wears them proudly every day and tells everyone how God has provided for him.

In Matthew 6:19, Jesus says, "Do not store up." Yet that's our modus operandi in America. We are "stuffocating" ourselves. We're living in a land of "affluenza." About half of the people who rent storage units do so not as a tool during times of transition, but simply as a permanent place for their extra things, even though the average home size has nearly doubled in recent decades. In the 1950s the average house size was 983 square feet. Today, the average house is nearly 2,300 square feet. Back in the fifties only 1 percent of houses had more than four bedrooms (even when the families were larger). Today, 34 percent of homes have four or more bedrooms (even when families today are smaller). Less than 1 percent of houses had a two-car garage, and now 81 percent of homes do—if not more than two. And for many of us, we leave our cars parked in the driveway because we have too much stuff piled in the garage.

Even with all this space in our houses, bedrooms, and garages, 20 percent of Americans have possessions in rented storage units! Today, there are reality TV shows that expose the massive amounts of clutter people have accumulated in their homes.

All this stuff isn't healthy, and it doesn't last anyway. "Do not store up for yourselves treasures on earth," Jesus says, "where moth and rust destroy and where thieves break in and steal. But store up for yourselves treasures in heaven where moth and rust do not destroy, and where thieves do not break in and steal. For where your treasure is, there your heart will be also."

I don't know what de-cluttering and de-accumulating will look like for you. Some people love to organize garage or yard sales. But if you sell your stuff, don't use the money to buy more stuff, or you'll be right back where you started. Instead, give it to a missionary, a single mom, a family in need, or someone who's unemployed. Use the cash for the glory of God. The more you do, the less of a hold it will have on you. Open your hands and you will experience the joy of living a generous life.

Jesus warned in Luke 12:15, "Watch out! Be on your guard

against all kinds of greed; a man's life does not consist in the abundance of his possessions." One of the best ways to drive this point home is to get rid of some of our abundance. Many de-clutterers give their stuff to family, friends, and neighbors. Or it goes to charities such as Goodwill or the Salvation Army. Where I live, if you just stick your stuff out in front of the house, it disappears like magic! Just put it out there and back away slowly. The next morning you'll find that it's gone.

One of my wife's friends took an interesting approach to de-cluttering. Her husband was a pack rat, and one time he was searching for a box that contained his utility bills from thirteen years earlier. Unable to find it, he asked his wife where they were. "Honey," she replied, 'fessing up, "I never told you, but last time we moved I put every third box in the dumpster that was parked near our house! So I guess you're not going to find that utility bill from thirteen years ago." But be warned, using this approach can be hazardous to your marital health and happiness.

However you choose to de-clutter and de-accumulate, be sure to follow through. Be ruthless with yourself. The more you do it, the easier it will get. And the payoff—in peace of mind, relief from stress, contentment, more space, blessing toward others, and eternal rewards—will dwarf any losses you might temporarily experience.

Worldly wealth counts for so much less than spiritual wealth (Revelation 3:17–18). In Mark 10:21–22, Jesus asked a certain rich man to make a choice: God or stuff.

Jesus looked at him and loved him. "'One thing you lack,'" Jesus said. "'Go, sell everything you have and give to the poor, and you will have treasure in heaven. Then come, follow me.' At this the man's face fell. He went away sad, because he had great wealth."

The man's face fell. Jesus wasn't being unkind. But He knew that this man was spending all of his time, energy, and money being consumed by his possessions. The reality is that if we are not careful, possessions can possess us. We can spend our time buying things, organizing things, storing things, using things, showing off our things, and wanting more things. The more possessions we have, the more possessions have us.

While the Lord doesn't ask everyone to sell everything, He does expect us to examine our heart. If anything is there other than Jesus, we need to remove it, immediately. One of God's greatest provisions to us is our very self, and it is a gift we should not take lightly. Our response to His provisions will tell us whether we are truly His disciples. "What good will it be for a man," Jesus asks, "if he gains the whole world and forfeits his soul?" (Matthew 16:26).

For groups, classes, or family discussions, choose the most interesting three to five questions to discuss together.

1. If you've successfully gotten out of debt (or are actively working at it), what practical steps did you have to take to get going in the right direction?
2. What is the worst financial advice you ever received? The best financial advice?
3. How do you think the "less is more" principle could be applied to your life?
4. When is the last time you did some serious de-cluttering and de-accumulating? How did it make you feel when you were all done?
5. If you sold some items you no longer needed, how could you use some of that money for the kingdom of God?

PART TWO
Receive God's Principles

Chapter 5

GOD-FIRST
PRINCIPLES

Recognizing God's provisions, as we have done in the first section of this book, is a great start to experiencing Him as our Provider. Walking with Jesus in this way is not an exercise in positive thinking or wish fulfillment. God is not a magical genie in a bottle who gives us everything we think we want or need. At the same time, we don't spiritualize this whole subject and hope for the best, not really expecting God to act in the real world. No, we are looking to honor God in our lives and to actually experience Him as our Provider. As the verses and stories I have shared have shown, we can trust God to break into this world and provide what we need, either miraculously or through "natural" processes. He is sovereign either way. But God also expects us to participate in His work, and in the first section we began to see what that looks like in the real world.

TRANSFER OWNERSHIP BACK TO GOD

In this part, "Receive God's Principles," we will home in on some vital truths that will guide us in this exciting faith journey and keep us on track. Colossians 1:16 states it clearly: "All things were created by him and for him." That's the first God-First Principle: Everything you and I have was created by God and for God. God's authorship of all things is followed by His ownership of all things. That only makes sense. Just as an author or inventor retains the copyright or trademark to his or her creations, so God retains the right to all His works.

The flip side of this truth is equally clear. If all things were created by God and for God, then we must face the fact that all things were not created by or for us.

This brings us to another truth found in the following verse: "He is before all things, and in him all things hold together" (Colossians 1:17).

Regarding God's power to maintain things, perhaps you have wondered how your vehicle has ever been able to keep running all these years. Remember that in Him all things hold together—even that old car! In 1 Chronicles 29:11, King David prays to the Lord and says, "Everything in heaven and earth is yours. You are exalted as head over all. Wealth and honor come from you."

If this is true, and Scripture affirms over and over that it is, then we need to respond to this God-First Principle. This is a fact that needs not only to sink into our heads but into our hearts and hands as well.

And when it sinks into our heads, hearts, and hands, we are prepared to do something radical: Transfer ownership of all we are and all we will ever have back to God. Transferring ownership is life changing and supremely logical. It's also a strategic spiritual act that transfers ownership of all we'll ever have back to its rightful Owner. Once we do this, we become managers and stewards of whatever God entrusts to us to utilize in the various seasons of our lives. The great missionary martyr Jim Elliot understood this well when he said, "He is no fool who gives what he cannot keep to gain that which he cannot lose."

A number of years ago I had the opportunity to speak to about thirty thousand men at some Promise Keepers events. I talked about God's ownership of all we have and the importance of being generous with whatever God gives us, and faithfully managing our God-given resources using biblical principles. At the end of the Promise Keepers events, it is common to call the men forward or ask them to stand where they are sitting to dedicate themselves to God. But the Lord led me to have them stay seated. I asked all thirty thousand men to reach into their pockets and take out their wallets or money clips and raise them up in the air. For those with nothing, I asked them to raise their empty hands up to God. I then led them in a prayer that we all prayed together phrase by phrase. Here was the prayer: "Heavenly Father, thank You that all I have and all I am comes from You. Thank You that all I ever will have and all I can ever be will come from You. Help me to generously share whatever you give me. Help me to faithfully manage all You entrust to me. From this day forward and every day the rest of my life. In Jesus' name, amen."

For many of those men, this symbolic act and congregational prayer may have been the first time they ever connected the spiritual dots that God was the true Owner and Provider of all they had and ever would have. On this day, with the help of the Holy Spirit, I am sure that God moved in some of their heads, hearts, and hands to make this a life-transforming experience.

When you transfer ownership back to God, you say, "God, all I have and all I ever will have belongs to You." Crown Financial

> *When you transfer ownership back to God, you say, "God, all I have and all I ever will have belongs to You."*

Ministries, a ministry I greatly admire and recommend, gives participants in their small group Bible study or Sunday school classes a "quit claim deed" on which they write down everything they have and then symbolically transfer it back to God and say, "From this point forward it all belongs to You." They then can sign the document. Some people also have others sign as a witness to this divine transaction. This is not only a logical and spiritual act, it's also incredibly freeing. Gone is the burden that you have to provide for yourself and take care of every problem on your own. When you sign things over to God in your heart or on a piece of paper, something happens inside and you stop grasping at things, open your hands, and say, "God, it's all Yours."

After one of the Crown classes at our church, a woman told me, "I'm a schoolteacher. I'm single and in my fifties. I've gone to bed every night of my life afraid."

"Afraid of what?" I asked.

"Afraid of my finances," she replied. "If I get sick or something happens to me, who is going to take care of me? Who is going to watch over me? I have always had this anxiety in my heart over how my life was going to go. Then I filled out that quit claim deed piece of paper. On the paper and in my heart, I turned my checkbook, savings account, health insurance, pension, car, and everything else over to God."

"An interesting thing happened," this schoolteacher continued. "I now go to sleep at night and don't worry about 'my stuff' anymore, because I know it's all God's stuff. I'm at peace, and I also have the sense that if something happens to me, God is the One who will take care of me because everything I have is God's, and I am God's. He is my ultimate Provider. This simple act has brought tremendous peace into my life that I have never before experienced."

To avoid the challenge of this kind of decision or simply because they haven't thought it through, sometimes people say, "That's all well and good, but I don't have anything to transfer back to God." College students often think they have nothing. One young lady heard a message about transferring ownership to God, and doubted she possessed anything of value. It finally dawned on her that she had a really good snowboard. So she said, "The only thing I have that's of any value is this snowboard." In her dorm room, she put the snowboard down, got on her knees, and said, "God, this snowboard is Yours. It's not mine. You use it however You want, but I want this snowboard to be used for Your glory." And do you know what happened in response to that prayer? God miraculously opened up a way for her to be coached by one of the leading snowboard coaches in America and she began training for the Olympics. But she knows that the goal in her life isn't gold medals but to give glory to God in everything she does and to be a witness for Him wherever she goes. As Jesus said, whoever seeks to save his life will lose it, but whoever loses his life for Him will find it (Luke 17:33). When you dedicate what you have to God—your house, your car, your clothes, your iPod, your whatever—something changes. When you transfer ownership to God, you receive freedom and grace that you can't get any other way.

While transferring ownership can be a special moment in your spiritual journey, the reality is that it is not a "once-and-done deal." Romans 12:1–2 says, "I urge you, brothers, in view of God's mercy, to offer your bodies as living sacrifices, holy and pleasing to God—this is your spiritual act of worship. Do not conform any longer to the pattern of this world, but be transformed by the renewing of your mind. Then you will be able to test and approve what God's will is—his good, pleasing and perfect will." When we daily offer our bodies to God, we are also offering Him all we are and all we have.

GIVE TO GOD FIRST

It is a good idea to sign a deed and to take a major first step to committing everything we are and have to God. But the proof of that transfer comes in the daily choices we make, in our lifestyle choices, in our purchases, in the spending plans (budgets) we put together, in the spending we do and don't do. It's one thing to say we believe that God owns it all. It's another to actually live that way. That's why the second God-First Principle I am going to discuss takes it to another level—give to God first as your highest financial priority.

The problem is, many people will draw back when faced with this challenge. They'll say, "Well, you don't understand my situation." Then come the reasons: "I'm unemployed." "I am on a fixed income." "I have kids in college." "I've got a lot of bills." "I've got to pay for my car." "I need to pay for my home." Such responses, which make sense on the surface, secular level, ultimately don't work because those who offer them indicate that they are the ones who don't understand.

When you learn to give to God first, He can stretch even the little amount you have to make it go further than you ever thought possible.

They may understand their financial situations, but they don't understand who God is. God is so much greater than a mortgage or a car payment, isn't He? Giving to Him first as our highest financial priority allows us to say, "God, I am recognizing You as the most important One in my life. Anything I have and ever will have, I will use to honor You first." It is not about giving God what is left, but learning to give to God what is right. When you try to give to God from the leftovers, there is usually nothing left. When you learn to give to God first, He can stretch even the little amount you have to make it go further than you ever thought possible. This kind of commitment to honor Him with our wealth fits with Psalm 67:7, which says, "God will bless us, and people all over the world will fear him" (NLT). The word *fear* can translate to "respect," "reverence," or "worship." The resources that you and I receive can go around the world and touch people for the glory of God. And God, the owner of it all, will provide.

An elderly woman at our church spent all of her working life serving on the staff of a Christian ministry. One day she asked me, "Do you know when I started giving to God?" I replied, "No, I don't, tell me the story." She said, "When I was eight years old, a speaker came to our church and gave away these little envelope systems, and I got one of them. So, whenever I would get a dime, I would divide it up into ten pennies, and put a penny in the first little envelope. God's envelope was on the top. That money was for missionaries. I started supporting missionaries as an eight-year-old by putting pennies in that little envelope. And I have never stopped. That was over eighty years ago."

She went on to tell me that when she started working with the ministry organization where she had served for decades, she only received room, board, and $5 per week for many years. And yet over her lifetime, she said every need was taken care of. A professional financial advisor recently told this ninety-year-old woman that she gives away too much money. "You need to take care of yourself," he warned. She told him, "I think God is taking better care of me than I can, so I don't want to slow down or stop my giving." "I guess you're right," this financial professional had to admit. "You're doing just fine."

Such giving runs counter to the world's wisdom, which whispers—even shouts—to us that it's all about taking care of yourself. This woman lives a life that truly honors God with her finances. Did you notice the first thing she did as an eight-year-old girl? She *set God's money aside.* She didn't commingle it with the other pennies. She set it aside and she specifically set it aside with a distinct plan and purpose to give it to God. To have used those set-aside pennies for any other purpose would have been the same as stealing from God. This is another great God-First Principle. Deuteronomy 14:22 says, "*Set aside* a tithe [a tenth] of all that your fields produce each year" (emphasis mine). In the Living Bible, the next verse says, "The purpose of tithing is to teach you always to put God first in your lives."

Not many of us are still farmers in the twenty-first century, but there is something important here that I don't want you to miss. While many Christians focus on the amount to give—and the amount is important—let's focus right now on the words *set aside*. This is the most important principle we can probably *ever* *learn* about becoming a generous Christian and learning to give to God. We must have a plan to actively set "God's money" aside.

You cannot commingle the money you believe God is calling you to give to Him with all of your grocery money, gas money, entertainment money, and anything else. If you do, every act of giving will induce pain. It will feel as if you're somehow getting shortchanged. But if you learn to give 10 percent (or more) to God, you will feel that the remaining 90 percent is enough. I once read a quote that said, "If you are a pauper and you learn to give to God, you'll feel like a prince. But if you're a prince and you don't learn to give to God, you will always feel like a pauper."

Ultimately, there are four S's that are the keys to you becoming and always being a generous person for the rest of your life. The first S is "Seeing" God's provisions in your life. The second S is using your hands to "Set aside" for the Lord what you are going to give. The third S is using your head to give "Systematically" what you've set aside. The fourth S is giving "Spontaneously" by being open-handed when God prompts your heart to give. God wants you to use your hands, head, and heart to become a generous person with whatever He gives and entrusts to you.

Like the eight-year-old girl, we each need to come up with a "system" that works for us. I know some people who keep separate line items in their spreadsheets, others who put God's money in a cookie jar, some who always make sure they write the very first check after they are paid to God, and more and more people are using electronic and online giving to make sure they "set aside" and faithfully give the first portion of their income to their church and the ministries God has called them to support. I tell people that if you "learn to faithfully set aside God's money, God will faithfully show you where to give it."

During the Great Depression, another friend, Pat, was about seven, and she asked her mother for a penny. Her mother replied, "Honey, we don't have a penny in this house." Pat answered, "Mom, yes we do!"

"Where do we have a penny?"

"In that drawer over there."

"What do you mean?"

"Well, in that drawer there's a little box. We've got over $2 in that box."

"Honey, that's God's money. That money doesn't belong to you, and that money doesn't belong to us. That's God's."

"Where'd you get that from, Mom?"

"Well, I went and worked ten days as a nurse for somebody who was very sick, and I got $30. When I came home I put $3 in that little tin, and that's God's money. We gave $1 of it away and now we still have $2 left to give."

"What about the rest of the money?"

"That's all gone, and we don't have a penny in this house for us."

Pat never forgot that. At age seven she understood that some things belong to God, even if we are facing tough times. May we understand the same thing. The lesson will be much easier if we set the money aside. In reality, of course, it all belongs to God— what we set aside and what we don't. Yet it is a discipline of faith to set that portion aside, trusting God to provide even as we put Him first.

God is very good at getting our attention in these matters because He knows us. Sometimes He uses the carrot; at other times, the stick. Sometimes, in His merciful wisdom, He uses both, as in Malachi 3:8–10.

"Should a person rob God?" he asks. "But you are robbing me. You ask, 'How have we robbed you?' You have robbed me in your offerings and the tenth of your crops. So a curse is on you, because the whole nation has robbed me. Bring to the storehouse a full tenth of what you earn so there will be food in my house. Test me in this," says the Lord All-Powerful. "I will open the windows of heaven for you and pour out all the blessings you need" (NCV).

Note here that first God uses the stick. His people are cursed because they have "robbed" Him. Treating God lightly with our finances can have negative consequences, then and now. Putting God first in our giving is not some optional extra only for super-spiritual believers. If we know we are to honor God with our wealth and choose not to, we cannot expect His blessings to remain upon us.

Of course, the primary party here is not us, but God. Malachi points out that failing to give to God is actually stealing from God.

Imagine if someone had been stealing from their employer for a number of years. Imagine they bought their house and car using this stolen money. Worse, the restaurant meals they ate and the vacations they enjoyed were also bought with the ill-gotten money. But one day they finally realized that stealing from your employer is not a very good idea. And then imagine this person came to my office when I was a pastor. "Pastor," he tells me, "I need to confess something. I've been stealing from my employer for a long time. As a matter of fact, I've built my lifestyle on this thievery. What do you think I should I do?"

Do you think as a pastor I would look the other way? Should I tell him in a soothing voice, "I understand you need this stolen money to support the lifestyle you've created for yourself"? Would I comfort him with the words, "Well, I know you really need the money. You're counting on it. You've built your whole way of life on it. There's no way you can stop cold turkey. How about this? Next week, just steal a little less. Don't steal quite as much as before. If you've been stealing $400 a week from your employer, how about cutting back to $350 for a while? Then, maybe in a month or two, you can get it down to $300. Perhaps in six months you'll reduce it to $200, and maybe in a year or two you might lower it to $100. And eventually you won't have to steal anything at all."

Does this make sense? Would I ever tell you, "Just steal a little less"? Of course not. Ultimately, following God means humbling yourself and learning to do what is right. You can then look to the Lord for grace and guidance in the journey. He's the one who will show you what to do. He will lift you out of the mud and mire of the slimy pit you've slipped into by years of wrong choices and habits.

I have sat and counseled with many people whose lives were in financial shambles. They would bring their income sheets, list of assets, budget, and list of debts into my office and many of them would be tens of thousands of dollars in debt. I would look at all the numbers and then I would ask them the following question: "From now on, whenever you get paid or get any money, are you willing to first give to God at least 10 percent or get more of what He's given you?" The frequent reply was, "What? Are you crazy? Look at the mess we're in. There is no way we're going to give to God first. First, we'll clean up this mess and then maybe we'll start giving something to God." I would then look at them and say, "I realize the mess you're in. Unfortuantely, there is no way to build you a spreadsheet plan that will help you eliminate this mountain of debt you've built for yourselves. The problem is so big that it will take all the help of heaven to get you out of this mess. You must have God's help to get out of it. And the only way I know to invite God and His help into this problem is to first honor Him with whatever He has given you. If you choose to do this, there is help and hope for your financial future. If you won't do this, I don't have any help I know that will work. So, what's your decision?" Over the years of counseling people, the decision has gone 50/50. Fifty percent of the people have said, "Okay, it sounds crazy to us, but if you really think God can help us out of the mess we've created, we'll go with what you're saying." The other 50 percent have replied, "No way and no thanks."

In these scenarios, I have seen God give grace to the humble and resist the proud. Over the years, many people who began to give to God first climbed out of the financial hole they were in within a number of months or a few years. Those who walked out the door to do it on their own have told me two and three years later that their financial problems were far worse than when they walked out of my office.

Normally, I don't use the word *tithe* very much because it usually sets off lots of theological arguments that go nowhere good. I do tell people that systematically and faithfully giving 10 percent or more to God is the starting block, not the finish line. I believe it is a good idea to start there but I don't necessarily believe God wants us to stay there. There are lots of faithful tithers who never become generous givers. In my own life's journey, I began to give to God the first 10 percent of my paycheck when I had more month than money. Over the years, there have been times when we've given 15 percent, 20 percent, and even 50 percent of our income to God. In recent years, we've lived on a five-figure pastor's income but have given a six-figure amount each year to God's work.

When we learn to give to God I believe we learn to experience God as our Provider. Sometimes this means that God stretches our meager resources, other times it may include Him providing for us in special and unexpected ways, and frequently it means He gives us godly wisdom so we don't make foolish choices or impulsive purchases with the money He's entrusted to us. When I began to be a faithful giver, I realized I was living beyond my means. God gave me the grace to sell my nice Chrysler Cordoba and get a little Ford Pinto. I stopped going on trips I couldn't afford. I stopped buying expensive clothes with a credit card that I was making minimum payments on. Did God provide? Yes. But much of His provision was grace, wisdom, courage, and guidance and not just unexpected cash or checks in the mail.

Second Corinthians 8:7 strengthens this point: "See that you also excel in this *guilt* of giving" (emphasis added). Actually, that's not what this Scripture says at all. It really says, "See that you also excel in this *grace* of giving" (emphasis added). Giving is not about guilt. It's about God's incredible grace in our lives. Before I began to understand all this, I was a taker. I believed it was more blessed to receive than to give. But God's grace and learning to live generously turned me from being a selfish taker to having great joy in being a generous giver.

One of the students attending a class on finances I was teaching at a local church was a beautiful woman who had been born with arms that were no more than small appendages on the ends of her shoulders. The woman was on welfare, but she was still trying to learn what the Bible teaches about finances and giving. In class she asked, "I don't have a job and I don't have any regular income; do you think I should still give?" I replied, "Yes, you should give from whatever God has given you."

"Well, that's not what the pastor told me."

"What did the pastor tell you?"

The pastor in question was sitting at the end of the table. This woman pointed at him and said, "He told me

> *I do tell people that systematically and faithfully giving 10 percent or more to God is the starting block, not the finish line.*

that as long as I wanted to give, I didn't have to actually give."

I turned to the pastor and asked him, "What are your thoughts?"

Suddenly a bit on the defensive, he replied, "Well, she's obviously very poor, is on welfare, and can't afford to give, so I don't think she should be expected to give."

"Pastor," the woman replied, "I am not a second-class Christian. Don't make me one. I now realize that if God has given me food stamps, then I'm going to somehow give from the food I get with my food stamps. If God has given me rental assistance, I'm going to somehow share my home."

The pastor, who meant well, got converted on the spot to understanding the grace of giving. That woman began to give to God, and soon she had stories of God's grace all over her life. In the coming months, He provided her with work, with her own home, with various creative provisions that met her needs. She was now well on her journey to experiencing the supernatural grace of giving (and receiving) in her life as she discovered God as her Provider.

Jesus said we can only serve one master—God or money (Matthew 6:24). How we handle money is a leading spiritual indicator of our faith. If we hold tightly to "our" money, it's a clear sign of spiritual trouble—like a warning light on the car dashboard. If this chapter makes you uneasy and uncomfortable, please sit up and take notice. The warning light is on. You likely have been missing out on God's best for you. He wants to help you learn to become a generous person and to experience more of His grace in your life.

One man said, "Until I learned to give to God, I was only playing church." He's right. If we're unwilling to give to God first as our highest financial priority, what makes us think we are really trusting God with our lives. We reap only what we sow (Galatians 6:7). How many people are merely filling pews in America today, playing church, because they've not learned how to honor God with what He has given them?

Someone experiencing a tough financial time recently told me, "We decided that when we get paid, the first check we write is to the Lord. We're not going to be sloppy. We want to honor the Lord with what He's given us even though our income has gone down." He is a world-class giver. Are you? Do you want to become one? In Genesis 28, Jacob was running away from home. He had a brother who had threatened to murder him, he had no job, he had no money, no possessions, and a very uncertain and scary future. But he had a dream and discovered in a fresh way that God was more real than he had realized growing up in his religious home. He immediately made the following vow to God in Genesis 28:20–22: "If God will be with me and will watch over me on this journey I am taking and will give me food to eat and clothes to wear so that I return safely to my father's house, then the Lord will be my God . . . and of all that you give me I will give you a tenth."

Have you made a Jacob decision yet? Have you prayed and said, "Lord, from this point forward, whatever You give me, whether it is little or much, I promise to give a tenth to You?" And if you have done this, are you growing in the grace of giving? Are you joyfully and generously increasing the percentage and the ways you are generously giving to God's work and to the needy? For each of us, our greatest acts of generosity are still ahead of us because God wants us to learn to become generous people and to continue to excel in the grace of giving.

For groups, classes, or family discussions, choose the most interesting three to five questions to discuss together.

1. Share a real-life story about how you first learned or put into practice that God is the Owner of everything you have. If this hasn't happened yet, are you willing to symbolically hold your open hands, purse, or wallet and pray the prayer (page 83) that I led men to pray at Promise Keepers conferences?
2. Is there a particular skill, interest, hobby, or ability you possess that you could intentionally dedicate to God and His use? What is it? How could this be used for God and by God to bless others and reach others?
3. If you actively "set aside" your giving to God's work, how do you practically do this?
4. Do you think there are any situations where people are exempted from the privilege of giving to God from whatever little or much they have? What would those be?
5. Have you made a "Jacob decision" in your life in which you determined that based on the reality of who God is, you would give 10 percent or more of your income to the Lord's work? If yes, when did this first occur and what was your financial situation at that time?

Chapter 6

PROTECTION PRINCIPLES

Putting God first in our finances is a worthy goal. For the Christian, it's also a necessary goal. Spiritual growth in your financial life will not come without this very basic step. It's one thing to say God owns it all and we are going to give in a way that reflects this truth, but it is another thing entirely to put God-First Principles into practice.

The difficulty comes because of three important truths about human beings: (1) We are fallen, (2) we are fallible, and (3) we have experienced failure in our lives. We start off with the best of intentions but somehow never reach our goals. Most Christians would want to experience God as their Provider. Most would even say they want to put God first in their finances. Somehow, though, it

> *Financial statistics regularly indicate that the average American spends more money than they take in.*

never seems to happen. Some financial problem always seems to block the way. That problem is us. Our fallibility, fallen nature, and past failures conspire to keep us from God's best. As the cartoon character Pogo said, "We have met the enemy and he is us." We need protection—from ourselves. That's what this chapter is all about.

In chapter 4 I talked about the necessity of adjusting your lifestyle to live below your means. This is a good idea not only because you will have the resources to give to God, save for the future, and meet your daily needs, but you will also better avoid the pitfalls of your fallibility, fallenness, and past failures. We've looked at the fact that Proverbs 21:20 tells us, "The wise man saves for the future, but the foolish man spends whatever he gets (TLB)." If only we in America were as disciplined as the foolish man! We're actually less so, because most of us not only spend right up to the limits of our income, but beyond them. Many people are driving down a winding financial mountain road with no guardrail protecting them from flying off the road and crashing. Our houses and cars are too big, and our bank balances are too small. Financial statistics regularly indicate that the average American spends more money than they take in. No wonder our balance sheets don't balance and we are getting hammered by interest on consumer debt!

Sometimes we look at the goal of putting God first and see the shambles that are our finances, and we throw up our hands, uncertain about what to do to get headed in the right direction. The problem seems too big to be solved. But that isn't the problem. The problem is simple: We spend too much. The solution is simple too. We need to learn to spend less.

I once counseled a couple who had just returned from a $1,200 getaway. They had put the entire amount on their credit card because "we don't have the money." They told me they needed the time away because of all the stress in their marriage due to their "financial problems." As I talked with them about developing a debt payback plan and a spending plan (i.e., a budget), I suggested that if they wanted to take a trip like this every year they would need to save $100 per month.

With shocked looks on their faces, they protested, "But we can't afford to save $100 a month for this type of trip every year. We don't make that kind of money!" I replied, "If you can't afford to save that amount of money, then you certainly can't afford the credit card and interest payments." No wonder this couple was experiencing financial stress!

There are ways, of course, to get needed R&R without busting the budget. Because of some financial emergencies that had come up, one family I know realized they didn't have the money available for their usual summer camping trip. So instead of going on a vacation they decided to have a "staycation." They parked their pop-up camper in their driveway at home, set up some tents on the lawn, and slept in them every night. They cooked out every day with the grill and found free concerts, museums, and events in their own city. A little unusual, perhaps, but years later, guess which vacation their kids talked about and remembered the most?

I know of other families who can't afford to take a vacation, but instead volunteer to help at a Christian camp for a week or two. All their meals and lodging are provided in a beautiful setting and their children can enjoy all the camp amenities.

The solution will look different for every person or family, although everyone must work out a plan with God's help to live below their means and still accomplish the things they know God would want them to do.

One idea I have shared with people is the 10-10-80 plan. That's not a long-distance calling plan, it's a quick and easy way to start living below your means. When someone uses this approach they give a tenth to God, a tenth (in savings) to themselves, and then they adjust their lifestyle choices to live on the rest. This approach will not be right for everyone, but it illustrates one way to begin to move forward.

The key is to start moving forward. And, as I have said, we may learn that some of our previous lifestyles and financial commitments no longer mesh with our newfound desire to give to God, and we may have to cut back. This can be a humbling process, but you will not be alone. I've known people who have come to this realization and then changed houses, cars, eating habits, entertainment, activities, and more. But for each of them, the reward has been great. Jesus said, "No one who has left home . . . or fields for me . . . will fail to receive a hundred times as much in this present age . . . and in the age to come, eternal life" (Mark 10:29–30).

DETERMINE WHAT YOU CAN AFFORD TO SPEND

Another Protection Principle is to predetermine what you can afford to spend on any item.

Once, Sandi and I went to a car dealer and we had $10,000 available in our checking account to buy a newer car. I told the salesman, "We want to get the best car we can for $10,000." The salesman replied, "What kind of monthly payment do you want?" and I said, "None." So he went over our numbers and we looked at some cars. Then he asked, "Now, how much monthly payment can you afford?" I answered, "No, we're not going to buy a car on payments. I would like to write a check for $10,000 to you or another car dealer and drive away with a car."

"But how much per month do you want to pay?"

"No, we're going to write a check for the full amount, because we don't want a monthly payment."

He couldn't get it—or maybe he just wouldn't get it. The salesman didn't want to sell me a $10,000 car. He wanted to sell me a $20,000 car. The problem wasn't the amount we had available to spend. I'm sure that if we had $20,000, he would have tried to sell us a $30,000 or $40,000 car. He wasn't being evil. He was looking out for himself. But when we're shopping for something, we need to be prepared. We need to determine how much we want to spend or someone else will talk us into how much they think we can afford to spend. Guess what? We walked out of the dealership without a car! They actually never showed us a car we could purchase with our $10,000 check. So we went to some other dealers and eventually found the car we wanted for the amount we predetermined we were willing to pay.

I've known many couples who were talked into buying a house by a realtor or a mortgage lender that required both of their salaries or far too much of their income.

Buying more car or more house than you can afford is a budget buster. People will listen to a mortgage broker, car dealer, or real estate agent who will try to talk them into buying far more than they can really afford. That's why we must use what the Bible calls in Deuteronomy 25:13 "accurate scales and honest measurements"(TLB) when it comes to building our spending plan (budget).

When you or someone else says you can devote 50 to 60 percent of your income toward a house, or 15 to 30 percent of your income toward a car, you're using dishonest scales. You can't do that *and* pay for all your other expenses and give to God. The famous baseball player and coach Yogi Berra once said, "Baseball is 90 percent physical and half mental." When it comes to your income, you only have 100 percent, not Yogi Berra's 140 percent. And with your 100 percent you'll need to give to God, pay taxes, save, and live your life. It's humbling to ask, "Lord, what have You provided?" Once you face those numbers—using honest scales— only then can you make good spending decisions. Once you know what you can afford while putting God first and living below your means, you can come up with a realistic budget for a house, your transportation needs, and so on.

One time I was teaching a class in India for a week to a group of adults on what the Bible teaches about finances. It turns out that the average income of the people in the class was $20 per month. I gave them an assignment to make a spending plan for a family of four that would cover giving to God, saving something for the future, shelter, food, clothing, transportation, education, and miscellaneous personal needs. Guess what? They didn't complain and say it was "impossible." All my groups of students came up with how this could be done with God's help. Many people say they have too little to manage. But in God's economy, the less you have, the more important it is to manage it well. The answer is *not* "more"; the answer is first learn to "manage" what you have. Scripture says that if you are "faithful in little things, you will be faithful in large ones" and "if you are dishonest in little things, you won't be honest with greater responsibilities" (Luke 16:10 NLT). The popular conference speaker Zig Ziglar says, "If you can't learn to be generous when it is hard, you'll never be generous when it is easy."

AVOID OR ELIMINATE
INDEBTEDNESS AND SURETY

If you do this kind of honest, hard-headed analysis, you will be well on your way to following another Protection Principle, which is avoiding or eliminating indebtedness and surety. Avoid indebtedness, or if you are already in debt, work to eliminate it. This includes all forms of consumer debt and other financial obligations. Surety is similar. Surety is a biblical concept that means you are taking on an obligation with no sure way to pay. An example of violating the surety principle would be buying groceries or any consumable item when you know you don't have the money in your bank account to pay the bill in full when it comes. When buying a house, it means that if you can't make the house payment, you not only lose the house but you will still have a financial obligation to pay even after the house is taken away from you. Many people who have had their homes foreclosed on in recent years were violating the principle of surety when they got interest-only loans or a bigger house than they could afford. Their ignorance of God's teaching on this subject brought a lot of hurt into their lives that they could have avoided if they had known and followed God's financial principles found in the Bible.

I once knew a woman who bought a used car and was being charged a 35 percent interest rate. When I worked with her to return the car after she had it for one year, the car loan agency said she needed to give them the car back and an additional $5,000. This purchase she made violated the surety principle. The same thing happens when someone buys a new car with a little down and years of monthly payments. As soon as they drive it off the lot they've violated the principle of surety. If after buying it they drove it one block and tried to return it, they would be told the car has now depreciated over the last ten minutes and is now worth thousands less than they had just paid.

Why should we go to all this trouble to avoid indebtedness and surety? Proverbs 22:7 says why: "The rich rule over the poor, and the borrower is servant to the lender."

The Bible does not say we cannot borrow, but it does say that those who do are slaves to their obligations. Speaking from personal experience, I have discovered that working to become debt free means you're free to follow the Lord's leading to do whatever He wants you to do and to go wherever He wants you to go. You're never tangled up by debts and financial obligations that keep you tied down. In my own life, I have traveled to over thirty-five countries and have ministered to thousands of people. One of the big reasons for this is that I have lived my life debt free for many years and I am free to serve the Lord however He leads. So many people are instead living the reality of the bumper sticker, "I owe, I owe, so off to work I go."

Before I became a pastor, I made a six-figure salary. Then I felt God's call into pastoral ministry, which pays a lot less than the business world. But I was free to follow that call because we had no mortgage, owned our cars, and were debt free. Ultimately, I took about a 65 percent pay cut to be a pastor, but this was no problem. We were financially free—free to serve God however He called. The truth is that anyone can experience a similar financial freedom by learning to avoid or eliminate growing indebtedness and surety.

> *I have discovered that working to become debt free means you're free to follow the Lord's leading to do whatever He wants you to do and to go wherever He wants you to go.*

"I am so mad," one pastor told me. "I went to Bible school. I went to seminary. I was a youth pastor, and I was in church every Sunday. But I never heard biblical truth on finances. By the time I was in my thirties, my wife and I were in $240,000 worth of debt and had nothing to show for it. Our life was a financial mess. Then five years ago I went through a Crown Financial Ministries financial class and realized I didn't have to live this way. Today, everything in our life is paid for. We own everything we have, we're content, we don't owe anyone a dime, and we are now giving 35 percent of our income to the Lord's work."

While doing guest speaking at a church recently one man told me that three years ago he and his wife went through Dave Ramsey's *Financial Peace University* class. He said that through this class they received the inspiration and instruction on how to become debt free. He told me that in the last three years they had paid off $65,000 in debts. Then six months ago, with only a thirty-day warning, the company where he had worked for thirty years let him and a bunch of his coworkers go. He told me that he was so glad he had paid off all those debts. He could sleep at night without worrying and while others were panicked and afraid he had God's peace in his life.

Whatever indebtedness you might be carrying—from credit cards, medical bills, student loans, mortgages, or car payments—you can probably be 100 percent debt free, including your house, within three to ten years, just by being intentional. But you have to want to reach that place of higher ground, of freedom, where it's all about serving the Lord. There are many ways to get there. As I mentioned, Dave Ramsey and Crown Financial Ministries classes and counselors can be a big help in getting you down the road of paying off your debts. The key thing is to decide on a plan and get started. By learning to be intentional, you don't have to live with that constant strain of bills, indebtedness, and surety. Instead of being a financial slave, you can be free to give, free to be the person God wants you to be and doing the things God wants you to do.

One way to look at this is to answer the question, "Is the Master in charge of your life, or is the MasterCard?" You will have to answer that question for yourself, but I can testify that the Master has taken far better care of me than the MasterCard ever did.

However, if you simply continue drifting along and doing the same old thing, don't be surprised if things get worse instead of better. Deuteronomy 28 warns, "If you refuse to listen to the Lord your God. . . . the foreigners living among you will become stronger and stronger, while you become weaker and weaker. They will lend money to you, but you will not lend to them" (vss. 15, 43–44 NLT). When a society or a people or a family experiences growing indebtedness, it's a likely indicator someone is not listening to the Lord.

Scripture points out that pride is often at the root of growing indebtedness. "Your heart was filled with pride," Ezekiel 28:17 says,

"You corrupted your wisdom for the sake of your splendor" (TLB). While this verse references Satan, it is no stretch to say that the Tempter is behind much of the consumerism poisoning our culture. There's something about wanting a "wow" house, "wow" electronics, a "wow" car, or "wow" clothes. Just below the surface is the lie, "If I have these cool things, then I'm somebody." The Bible says you can literally corrupt God's wisdom for the sake of that "wow." Ezekiel goes on: "You defiled your holiness with lust for gain; therefore I brought forth fire from your own actions and let it burn you . . ." (v. 18).

I understand the idea of letting your foolish and prideful behavior burn you. In high school I played a game called "heads or tails." It involved two players and one quarter. One player would flip a quarter and the other one would try to guess the outcome by saying heads or tails. If you got it right, you got the person's quarter. If you got it wrong, you owed them a quarter. Like lots of gambling, it was random luck and kind of addicting. One day I was playing with my friend Dave. He had flipped and I guessed wrong and I owed him quarter. He then said, "Double or nothing." So, we did it again. I lost and now I owed him 50¢. We flipped again and I lost. Now I owed him $1. He said "double or nothing" and I kept losing—$2, $4, $8, $16, $32, and finally, before I stopped, I owed this guy $64. Guess what? For sixty-four school days he came to my locker to collect his dollar. I learned that foolish pride in gambling can burn you and it cured me from ever wanting to gamble again.

Indebtedness can burn you. Many people have bought cars, electronics, and houses they really couldn't afford, and their finances, faith, and families have suffered because of it. They made unwise and unbiblical choices and have gotten burned.

STEER CLEAR OF FINANCIAL TEMPTATIONS

This brings us to the next Protection Principle: Steer clear of financial temptations. Psalm 119 puts it like this: "Turn my heart toward your statutes and not toward selfish gain. Turn my eyes away from worthless things" (vv. 36–37).

A few years ago someone invited me to a home show. My immediate response: "I can't afford to go."

"You don't understand," my friend said. "I have free tickets for you."

"No, it has nothing to do with the price of the tickets. I can't afford to look at all the cool things you can do to a house, because I can't afford to buy them. I like my house, and if I go to the home show there are going to be lots of things I will see that I will probably like and end up wanting. So, I can't afford to go."

The Bible tells us to flee temptation, and for that reason many people would be wise to admit that they "can't afford" to go to the mall, car show, electronics store, gun show, RV show, and any other place that will make them just want what they don't have. If people thought about it, they can't afford to easily put themselves in those places because they will end up being discontented with what they have and wanting what everyone is trying to sell them. When I was a child, my sister and I use to call the JCPenney catalog the "Wish Book." We would carefully look at all the toys, games, and sports stuff and want, want, want (or in our case, wish, wish, wish).

If someone has a problem with drinking, it probably is not wise to go to the bar or the liquor store. If a person has a problem with drugs, they shouldn't hang out with certain people or go to certain places. What is the financial Achilles' heel in your life? Whatever it is, learn to avoid the people or situations that cause you to be discontent and to want more.

In Genesis 3:6 it says, "When the woman *saw* the fruit of the tree was good for food and pleasing to the eye . . . she took some and ate it. She also gave some to her husband, who was with her, and he ate it" (italics added).

There's something about seeing something—seeing it on the shelf, seeing it in someone else's house, seeing someone else drive

> *What is the financial Achilles' heel in your life? Whatever it is, learn to avoid the people or situations that cause you to be discontented and to want more.*

it down the street. It's no accident that the tenth commandment tells us not to covet, wanting the same things that belong to others. Titus 2:12 says, "We are instructed to *turn from* godless living and sinful pleasures. We should live in this evil world with wisdom, righteousness, and devotion to God" (NLT, italics added). The apostle John talks about the lust of the eyes and the pride of life (1 John 2:16). Seeing can be deadly to your spiritual health, so ask God to help you navigate away from financial temptations in your life.

In our world, gambling and lotteries are a growing obsession with many people. As times get worse, more and more people think the hope for their future lies in a little scratch card. I often say that lotteries are a tax on people who are bad at math. If a person is looking for hope and happiness from a lottery ticket, they are scratching in the wrong place. Once in a gas station convenience store the woman ahead of me purchased $60 in lottery tickets. She then took the cards to a table and used a quarter to do the scratch off. Suddenly she looked all excited and said, "I won, I won!" I asked her, "How much did you win?" "Sixteen dollars!" She had just spent $60 and was rejoicing that she had won $16! I wanted to tell her that if she considered that to be "winning," I would meet her at the convenience store every day and hand her $16 for her $60. But I knew such a comment would be unkind and unwise.

Many people are oblivious to the moral and financial harm to themselves and others as they try by hook or by crook to "get ahead." Proverbs 13:11 says, "Dishonest money dwindles away, but he who gathers money little by little makes it grow."

We need to return to the old-fashioned idea that money grows little by little through hard work. Yes, the temptation to cheat is ever-present, but the results won't last. Proverbs 20:17 notes, "Some men enjoy cheating, but the cake they buy with such ill-gotten gain will turn to gravel in their mouths" (TLB).

I've tasted that mouthful of sand. As I grew up, I was a taker. I took from my brother, my sister, my parents, and my employer in my teenage years. To me it was all about getting what I wanted for myself, and I would get it anyway I could, even by stealing from loved ones, stores, and employers.

The Bible says that when you steal, it's sweet for a moment, but it will become like a mouthful of sand. It certainly did for me. That grit is disgusting and embarrassing. Whether it's cheating on your taxes, taking things from an employer, or not being honest with your customers, God says, "Don't go there. It will only bring pain and heartache." It will—sooner or later. But just trying to stop is not enough. God tells us not only to stop doing the bad, but also to start doing the good. "If you are a thief, quit stealing," Ephesians 4:28 says. "Instead, use your hands for good hard work, and then give generously to others in need" (NLT). The reality is that I was a thief. Then God came, forgave me, and commanded me to use my hands for good, honest labor. Instead of remaining a taker, I became a giver. The Lord also had me make restitution to all the people that I could find that I stole from. Restitution is God's cure so you never steal again. Usually the person who steals thinks they are getting something for nothing. But when you make restitution you have to go to the person (which is pretty humbling), confess what you've done (which is hard), pay them back in full for what you've taken (which hurts financially), and then give another 25 percent on top of what you've taken (which is a gesture of repentance and good will that brings God's healing). Once you go through this process, you never want to take anything ever again! The good news is that God can redeem us from our fallenness, fallibility, and past failures. His transforming grace can turn a taker into a generous giver and a dishonest person into one who is trustworthy.

For groups, classes, or family discussions, choose the most interesting three to five questions to discuss together.

1. Share a story about a time when you made a foolish financial decision or purchase that you later regretted.
2. If you have taken steps to adjust your lifestyle or spending to eliminate debt or live below your means, what active steps did you take to do this?
3. Many of us have been in a situation where a salesman tried to talk us into spending more on an item than we could really afford to. What are some ideas on how you can avoid this trap the next time you're buying a car, house, or other expensive item?
4. How did you first learn about the dangers and foolishness of indebtedness?
5. What is a financial temptation that you know will be important for you to steer away from?
6. Do you know anyone who has been hurt by chasing after get-rich-quick schemes, stealing, or gambling? What did you learn about the pitfalls of these things by watching what happened in their life and family?

Chapter 7

POSITIVE
PRINCIPLES

Once we take stock of our own fallibility, fallenness, and failures, we have a fighting chance to get our financial houses in order. Once we learn to implement God's Protection Principles, we are ready to learn and use His Positive Principles. Remember, the goal is not to amass riches in order to live a better life (though increased wealth is often the result). Rather, it is to experience God as our Provider so that we will be prepared to honor Him and serve others. The first Positive Principle is this: Know your financial status and goals. This knowledge is especially important in uncertain times like these.

KNOW YOUR FINANCIAL
STATUS AND GOALS

Proverbs 27:23 warns, "Riches can disappear fast" (TLB). In recent years, millions of people have lost what they thought were secure jobs. Many people lost pension and investment funds almost overnight. The potential for future economic problems in our country is very likely for many years to come.

Recently I read that a major corporation decided that effective in three months, all retiree pension benefits for 22,000 surviving spouses of retirees would be eliminated. In this newspaper article, one man said, "If I die today, my wife gets a $117,000 pension. But if I die in three months, she gets $0." For decades these couples thought that their pension funds would take care of both of them until they died. Then almost overnight a new CEO comes in and makes a decision that will negatively impact tens of thousands of people for years to come.

Proverbs 23:4–5 in the Living Bible says, "Don't weary yourself trying to get rich. Why waste your time? For riches can disappear as though they had the wings of a bird!"

A few years ago, an accountant told me that one of his clients had placed all of his retirement assets into his company's stock. On the day this client had retired from his company, his retirement nest egg was worth $600,000. Then this well-known company encountered sudden, unexpected turbulence and public scandal. In one week this client's retirement stock portfolio went from $600,000 to $180—from six figures to three figures, a sickening drop of 99.97 percent.

Have you ever heard the phrase "money talks"? Do you know what is says? It says, "Good-bye, adios, sayonara, I'm outta here." Proverbs 23:4–5 in the Living Bible says, "Don't weary yourself trying to get rich. Why waste your time? For riches can disappear as though they had the wings of a bird!"

Riches disappear. Fast. This is true even if nothing bad or catastrophic happens. Just living your normal life will cause riches to disappear.

In your mind, determine how much income you've made annually in ten years. Take your annual income and multiply by 10. Even for those with modest salaries, the number quickly grows into the hundreds of thousands of dollars. How much money have you earned in the last decade?

Write that amount here: $ _____.

Now answer this question: How much is left? Probably not much! How much did you spend of that amount? How much did you give? How much did you save?

For many of us, we really have no clue where our money has gone and where it is going. One of the greatest reasons to get on top of your finances is so you will be able to tell your money where to go instead of asking where it went. Knowing your financial status and goals will help you prepare for the uncertainties and changes the future will certainly bring.

Proverbs continues with a warning: "The king's crown doesn't stay in the family forever" (27:24 TLB). In other words, if you have the kind of job where you have a business card, your business card and title will change in the future. Seemingly secure things can and do change—and not always for the better. In fact, the only certainty in our economy is change. One of the most fearsome problems with what pundits are calling the Great Recession is the probability that many jobless people will not be able to find work paying anywhere near what they made before. Those jobs are, as they say, gone with the wind. We cannot count on what we have enjoyed continuing indefinitely. There are no guarantees.

This section of Proverbs also includes this advice: "So watch your business interests closely. Know the state of your flocks and your herds" (v. 4 TLB). How are your flocks and herds? What is your income? What are your assets? Your liabilities? Your lifestyle expenses? Your giving? How much are you spending, and how much of that spending is really necessary? How about your debts? How much are they, when will they be paid off, and at what interest rate? It is so important to be honest with yourself so you don't become self-deceived.

When I meet with people in financial trouble, I will not counsel them until they put together information and documents on their income, spending, assets, and bills. One couple refused to do this and told me that they only wanted to come in to see me so I could feel sorry for how big of a mess they were in. But if a person doesn't know their own financial status and goals, there is no way they can know where they are and know how to get where they want to go. It would be like trying to use a map, but you're not sure where you are and you're not sure where you want to go. If you aim at nothing, you're bound to hit it.

So this Positive Principle is to do the hard but necessary work of digging through your checkbook and your statements so that you have a solid understanding of your flocks and herds (income, expenses, assets, debts). Let's face it: If you don't do it, no one else will.

Most people go through life clueless about what's really going on with their flocks and herds and so are unprepared when the unexpected happens. Notice that I said *when* the unexpected happens, not *if*. Proverbs 21:5 tells us what will happen if we do keep an eye on our financial livestock: "Good planning and hard work lead to prosperity" (NLT).

The problem is, in America today, the average person comes into retirement with twenty or more years left on his or her mortgage and very little in the bank. It's no wonder that more and more Americans are forced to work during their so-called Golden Years.

So think through what is going on with your finances, look at what's ahead, and begin to prepare.

This can seem overwhelming, but there are people and resources available to help. In this book, I have mentioned Dave Ramsey and Crown Financial Ministries as good places to start. I also wrote a helpful manual called the *Because I Love You Family Organizer* that is filled with helpful forms that can help you get your financial house in order. Act in faith, not in fear, even if you sense it is late in the game. Trust as you move ahead that the Lord will give you wisdom and help.

SHARE WITH PEOPLE IN NEED

But as you seek God's provisions for yourself, please don't forget to be God's instrument to provide for others. The next Positive Principle: Share with people in need. It's not only good and right to be generous, but it opens the door to even more of God's blessings for us. Proverbs 22:9 puts it this way: "Generous people will be blessed, because they share their food with the poor" (NCV).

A number of years ago a study asked, "Are you rich?" People who answered no, and that was most of them, were asked a follow-up question: "Who's rich?" People making $25,000 a year said that those making $50,000 are rich. Those making $50,000 said people making $100,000 are rich. People making $100,000 said those making $250,000 are rich. Are you sensing a trend here? It goes on. People making $250,000 said people making $500,000 are rich. People making half a million dollars pointed to the people making a million. But surely the millionaires thought they were rich? No, they pointed to those making $2 to $3 million. Almost no one felt rich, whether making $25,000 or nearly 100 times that. Why? Could it be that they were comparing themselves with the wrong people?

What is the key to really feeling rich? Instead of looking up at those with more than you have, look around you; look at the people living on the other side of the tracks or the other side of the world. Decide to do something to help the needy and the less fortunate. Instead of watching television, keeping up with the Joneses, and getting ensnared by our consumer culture, help someone who really needs help. Suddenly, you'll realize how rich you are. In helping others, you will be helped yourself. There is a gratefulness, a thankfulness, and a grace that will come upon your life. Sandi and my teenage son, Josh, saw houses in Romania when they were visiting there for a missions project that were no more than hovels. They helped feed hungry and hurting people. Do you think they felt rich when they got home? When Sandi and I have returned from ministry trips to India, we usually find we don't have any urge to buy anything beyond the basic necessities for a number of months. This is because we realized in a tangible way how much we already have. People just as good, godly, and faithful as we are, are dying because they don't have enough. Many of us in the West, however, are dying because we have too much.

James 1:27 points out, "The Christian who is pure and without fault, from God the Father's point of view, is the one who takes care of orphans and widows" (TLB). The word translated as "widows" can also mean single women, single mothers, or lonely women. Think about it. This is an amazing verse. When we help the truly needy, God sees us as faultless.

One day I was talking with a boy at church. For some reason the subject of milk came up in our conversation, and he commented that he really missed being able to drink milk. I asked him what he meant and he said, "Ever since my dad was sent to prison, mom says we can't afford to have milk in the house." He was one of six young children, from two years old to nine years old, of a single mom whose husband was in prison. A few days later I read in Matthew 10:42 that Jesus said, "If anyone gives even a cup of cold water to one of these little ones because he is my disciple, I tell you the truth, he will certainly not lose his reward." I was struck by the verse. Even giving a cup of cold water would be recorded, remembered, and rewarded by God when we get to heaven. I talked with Sandi and we decided to buy this family a year's supply of milk that would be delivered to their door every week. If God rewards people for a cup of water, I know He will also reward us for giving some gallons of milk every week!

Another time I was praying and reading my Bible in the morning and the same family came to my mind. The Lord prompted me, "Give them your car." Give them my car?! I had a fairly new station wagon that I really liked that also got good gas mileage and was fully covered by a warranty. But our church was actively helping this family with their needs and I knew they had some type of vehicle that was costing a lot of money for gas. So I mentioned to Sandi, "I think God wants me to swap my station wagon with this family for whatever vehicle they are driving." Sandi told me she thought it was a good idea, and then commented with a smile, "Just don't give away my minivan!"

Then the phone rang and an acquaintance from the Christian camp where Sandi and I had served many years before called me on the phone. He was calling to get my financial advice. His truck was beyond repair and he needed to get a different truck. Some people were telling him to trust God for the payments and get a newer truck. But he wanted to know what I thought. I told him that this would be violating the biblical principle of surety because he would be taking on a financial obligation with no sure way to pay for it. He asked what he should do and I said, "Let's pray about it. If this is really a need, God has a way to provide it." Before we prayed I asked what type of truck he needed and he said it would be best if it was four-wheel drive and had an enclosed back.

So, I prayed with him and hung up. I then called the single mother and told her that we were sensing God wanted us to swap our station wagon for whatever she was driving. She quickly accepted the offer and I drove my car over to her house with the title and extra keys. (Note: When you own something outright without any debt, it is easy to give it away if God prompts you to do so.) She gave me her title and the keys and told me the Suburban she drove was in front of the house. While I was driving it home I thought to myself, "I don't want a big Suburban truck." And then I thought of Steve who I had talked and prayed with in the morning. I realized that this truck would be perfect for him, but he lived a thousand miles away in Wisconsin. I was listening to the radio as I was driving the Suburban home and the news came on and said a major winter blizzard was going to hit Colorado that night and that by morning the Colorado airports would shut down.

> *If we are godly, we will be generous, because God is generous. Generosity reflects the character of our heavenly Father.*

Well, the next morning I was scheduled to fly to Wisconsin to do guest preaching at a church. I suddenly realized that I wasn't going to be able to make it to Wisconsin on the plane, but I thought I could drive there that night ahead of the storm. I got home and my wife agreed with the plan, and we loaded up our family and luggage and outran the winter blizzard. We arrived safely in Wisconsin where we freely gave Steve this four-wheel drive, closed-back truck that we had prayed God would provide. But our family was now in Wisconsin without a car. However, we had been praying for a good friend who got laid off and who had been trying to sell his car for a number of months with no takers. But we had enough money in our checkbook to pay the price our friend needed for his car. So within forty-eight hours, four families were blessed by God. A single mom with six children got a newer station wagon, our prayer for a truck for Steve was answered, our friends were able to sell their car to us to generate cash they really needed for their family, and our family got a newer car!

The reality is that God wants us to be concerned for the least, the lost, and the lonely. We are to be "Jesus with skin on" to be a blessing to others with the blessing God has given us.

Second Corinthians 9:9 says that godly people "share freely and give generously to the poor. Their good deeds will be remembered forever" (NLT). If we are godly, we will be generous, because God is generous. Generosity reflects the character of our heavenly Father. There are no exceptions to this rule. If we are not generous, we are not godly. If we are not godly, we do not belong to Him.

SCHEDULE TIME TO
MANAGE YOUR FINANCES

The third Positive Principle is this: Reserve time in your schedule to manage your finances. This follows naturally from the first two. We have to know our financial status and goals, and we must give generously to those in need. Only then, with these foundations in place, are we ready to take control of our finances. And this third principle reminds us that we must be persistent and disciplined about it. Just as we set aside money to give, so we need to set aside time to manage our money.

Many people spend more time planning a vacation than they ever spend managing their finances. Keeping track of expenses, monitoring your giving so you are faithful to the Lord, checking your income, establishing financial goals, and tracking any investments will all take some time.

We're usually pretty good at spending our resources, but we're not always so good at managing them. Proverbs 13:16 says, "A wise man thinks ahead; a fool doesn't, and even brags about it!" (TLB). Let's be wise, not foolish.

We live in a world where people are buying on impulse and spending without thought.

First Corinthians 16:2 gives us a "minimal standard" for monitoring how God has provided for us and faithfully setting aside money to give to God at least once a week. The verse says in the Living Bible, "On every Lord's Day each of you should put aside something from what you have earned during the week, and use it for this offering. The amount depends on how much the Lord has helped you earn." One version of this verse I came across years ago said that each of us is to give according to how God has prospered us. Our Provider God wants us to clearly recognize and even record *how* He has provided for us, and then in a spirit of gratitude for His provisions, we are to faithfully and generously set aside offerings to give to the Lord's work.

At first, I didn't understand how the verse could apply to my life. But my wife and I began a Sunday evening practice of "looking back and writing down" how God provided for us in the previous seven days. Each week, we discovered there were many ways that God provided for us outside of our normal income. We began giving 10 percent of my main income to our local church and we then started a "Blessings Fund" that represented 10 percent or more of the myriad of blessings God creatively brought into our life week by week. At the end of the first year, even though my main income only brought in $15,000, I discovered we had given $1,500 to our local church and an additional $2,500 out of our "Blessings Fund" to other Christian causes. This meant that God had blessed us with $25,000 of blessings during the past year that was over and above my $15,000 salary! We did this for several more years and discovered that each year God doubled and tripled what we were able and willing to give to the Lord's work because we counted our blessings.

Here are the steps we followed and practiced that helped us live a more joyful and generous life based on clearly understanding how God provided for us week by week.

1. Plan a time each week where you will begin to write down God's provisions from the previous week in a "Blessings Notebook." In our case, we would do this on Sunday nights.

2. When you meet together, think back over the following areas and write down on paper or on a computer anything that comes to your remembrance from the following categories.

- **Main Income**—If you were paid during the week, write down that amount. For us, we gave 10 percent of this amount to our local church.
- **Additional Income or Unexpected Cash**—Write down any cash gifts, overtime pay, bonuses, second salary, moonlighting, investment returns, sale of any possessions, refunds, inheritance, etc.
- **People's Hospitality**—Meals, lodging, or entertainment that others gave to you or paid the cost.
- **Special Help or Assistance**—Help with car, house, equipment repairs, free babysitting, etc.
- **Discount or Sale Items**—Any money saved on discounted clothing or household items, garage sale/thrift shop savings, discounts on recreational activities, etc.
- **Purchase of New Possessions**—When my wife and I were buying a major item, we sometimes included the cost of these items in our Blessings Fund in order to help us be able to be more generous and give an additional 10 percent or more to the Lord's work.

3. Write down the financial value for each item *or* (very important) write down the amount you "would have been willing to spend" for the item. For example, a family member gave me a $1,000 radial arm saw. I would have never been able or willing to afford a $1,000 tool like this, but I might have "been willing to

spend" $200 on a used radial arm saw at a garage sale. So, in this example, I put down the value of the blessing at $200 (not $1,000).

4. Add up the value of the total number of blessing items for the week and take 10 percent or more of the total and decide where to give it, *or* set aside the week's amount in a notebook or put the money in a special account and consider this your "Blessings Fund."

5. Faithfully give your church 10 percent or more of your main income. Then begin to joyfully and generously use your "Blessings Fund" to help support missions, missionaries, special projects and needs, building programs, the needy, or Christian workers and organizations.

Over the years, we have shared this with many people and some have begun to practice something similar to this plan.

Here's my personal Four-Week Challenge to you: I am confident that the Lord has been blessing most people's lives week by week. But most people don't "see" the blessings because they don't take time to "look back over the last seven days to see what God has done to provide for them." Because of this, I challenge you to try this for at least four weeks to see what God is doing for you. I believe it will truly lead you to a more joyful and generous life.

Beyond counting your blessings and making sure you are setting aside offerings to be a faithful giver, also include time in your schedule to manage the rest of your financial matters. Proverbs 24:3 reminds us, "Any enterprise is built by wise planning, becomes strong through common sense, and profits wonderfully by keeping abreast of the facts" (TLB). Sounds like it was written yesterday, doesn't it? This verse applies to any enterprise, whether it is a Fortune 500 company, a crisis pregnancy ministry, or your family finances. A basic part of wise planning is simply sitting down and understanding the income and the outgo. Ask yourself some basic questions: Where is your income coming from (wages, salary, gifts, payments, interest)? Where does your income go (shelter, food, transportation, entertainment, miscellaneous)? Whenever possible, look for ways to involve your children in understanding your family finances. One of the reasons I wrote the *40 Day Spiritual Journey to a More Generous Life* is so families could learn, read, and discuss the biblical financial principles based on the four hundred Scripture verses found in this devotional. There are also weekly worksheets to help everyone in your family understand your income sources, lifestyle spending, assets and debts, and giving priorities. If you want them to begin experiencing God as their Provider, you need to teach and model the biblical principles we've been discussing.

It will also take some work. Yes, I know people are looking for financial security in five easy steps, for a secret no one has ever thought of, for their computers to make the money for them. But the fact is, God has designed us to work, and to profit from our work. Proverbs 14:23 says, "Work brings profit; talk brings poverty!" (TLB). We can talk all day and all night, but if we never get out of our chair and put our hand to the plow, we cannot expect to survive—much less prosper. That's why Paul warned, "If a man will not work, he shall not eat" (2 Thessalonians 3:10).

This is a hard word, but it is a gracious word. Some of us think that we are trapped in poverty or in our past mistakes. We feel powerless to change our circumstances. We blame our personal or family history, our personality, our lack of training and teaching on these subjects. It is time to move past the blame game and move on to biblical principles that can bring you the financial freedom you've heard about but maybe have never experienced yourself. We need to pray and act upon what the ancient Hebrews prayed to the Lord from Psalm 90:17: "May the favor of the Lord our God rest upon us; establish the work of our hands for us—yes, establish the work of our hands." We need to put our financial houses in order, so let us pray that same prayer. Our gracious Provider will answer.

For groups, classes, or family discussions, choose the most interesting three to five questions to discuss together.

1. How do you monitor your financial income, giving, spending, goals, and progress?
2. What are some financial goals you think would be good to have for the next year, three years, or ten years?
3. Do you consider yourself rich? Why or why not?
4. Do you know a single parent, fatherless child, widower, or foreigner that you could help in some way? Share some details about their life, how you know them, and how you could be of help to them.
5. What would be some advantages of "counting your blessings" every week and then giving offerings to God's work based on these financial and material blessings?
6. What were your thoughts about the station wagon and truck story (pages 117–118)?

Chapter 8

ETERNAL
PRINCIPLES

A s you have probably discovered by now, this is not a book of investment advice. I'm not going to tell you what stocks to pick, what investment philosophy to follow, what tax strategies to employ, or what asset allocation approach seems best given present and anticipated economic trends. There are many other places where you can get that kind of advice.

My goal is to help you experience God's riches in your life— riches that are available to all His children and that sometimes translate into increased standards of living, but not always. Jesus Himself drew a distinction between worldly wealth and true wealth. "So if you have not been trustworthy in handling worldly wealth," He asked, "who will trust you with true riches?" (Luke 16:11). Don't get me wrong, worldly wealth is important, at least some of the time. We need it to take care of our own and others, and to support the work of God's kingdom. As George Bailey asked Clarence the angel in the 1946 film *It's a Wonderful Life*:

"You don't happen to have eight thousand bucks on you?"

"Oh no, no. We don't use money in heaven."

"Comes in pretty handy down here, bub."

But Clarence was right to recognize the difference between worldly wealth and true riches. Whatever riches we have, God is our Source and Provider. Yes, He gives the resources necessary for life, but, even better, He gives peace, knowledge, wisdom, joy, understanding, contentment, and so many other things. Those are the "heart things." Money can't buy those things, but God can give them.

INVEST FOR ETERNITY

In this section of the book we have already learned God's Protection Principles and his Positive Principles concerning finances. Now it's time to learn His Eternal Principles. The first is this: Invest for eternity. What have you deposited in the First Bank of Heaven? First Timothy 6:17–18 breaks down the difference between worldly wealth and true riches. Let's walk through it. "Tell those who are rich not to be proud and not to trust in their money which will soon be gone" (vs. 17 TLB).

There is an old joke about a dying rich man who could not bear to part with his precious wealth, so he convinced an angel to let him take one suitcase worth of his riches, as he attempted to disprove the old adage, "You can't take it with you." So the day came and the rich man died. He showed up at the Pearly Gates toting his baggage, which was quite heavy. Saint Peter met him there, saying, "This is highly irregular!" But he checked the records and discovered that the man had received a special permission. "Okay, open it up," Saint Peter said. So the man did, revealing some tightly packed gold bars. Peter looked at the bars and then at the man, who was much chagrined by Peter's response: "You brought pavement?"

Of course, the truth is, you can't take it with you. "Do not store up for yourselves treasures on earth," Jesus said, "where moth and rust destroy, and where thieves break in and steal" (Matthew 6:19). Paul tells Timothy, "Tell them to use their money to do good. They should be rich in good works and should give happily to those in need, always being ready to share with others *whatever* God has given them" (v. 18 TLB, italics added).

What's your "whatever"? You're to give from whatever God has given you. Do you own a house? Maybe the Lord wants you to share it with someone who needs a place to stay. Do you have a car? Maybe the Lord wants you to give someone a ride to church, or to the doctor, or to the grocery store. Do you have food? Set aside some for a friend who's struggling. Do you go out to eat? Maybe the next time you visit a restaurant you can take someone you just met along. If you have clothes you no longer need or possessions you no longer use, give them to a thrift shop or a family in need.

> *This kind of abandon with "our" stuff can sound frightening, even intimidating. Actually, it's liberating and kind of fun!*

All of us must answer the question, "What has God given us?" and then share whatever it is. This kind of abandon with "our" stuff can sound frightening, even intimidating. Actually, it's liberating and kind of fun! God loves cheerful givers (2 Corinthians 9:7).

Once I was in India and I met some former Buddhist monks from Bhutan who had become Christians. One of the former monks had spent several years translating the Bible by hand into school notebooks into his native language. Now he was ready to print the Bibles, but he needed money to buy a computer to type in all of his handwritten notes into the software program. I wanted to help him, but I didn't have any cash at all. I was praying about how I could possibly help. The Lord prompted me in my heart, "Give him what you have." But I thought, I don't have anything. I don't even have a single dollar bill to give him. But the Lord spoke to me again, "Give him your computer." I realized this man did not need money, he needed a computer. But this laptop I had with me was a very expensive laptop and it had all my files on it. But after praying about it more, I knew that I could also come home and buy another computer but this Christian brother needed a laptop now. So I spent all night copying my computer files onto an external hard drive and at 7:00 a.m. I met him and gave him the computer just minutes before he and his friends were leaving to return to Bhutan. We joined hands and prayed, giving thanks to God for His provisions and for how this laptop computer was going to be used to give people in Bhutan a copy of the Bible in their own language. The brothers from Bhutan went away rejoicing because God had provided. And I went away rejoicing because God chose to use me and my "whatever" (my laptop) to help get a Bible to people who would become Christians who I would get to meet in heaven someday. I truly believe this act of being open-handed with my laptop was an investment in eternity.

A very wealthy businessman was known for his generosity. But the industry he made his fortune in plunged headlong into a terrible downturn. Suddenly, this Christian philanthropist lost great amounts of his personal wealth and in fact faced very difficult times. Hearing of his plight, some people came and asked, "What do you think about your giving now? Don't you wish you would have kept that money for yourself?" The man answered, with conviction, "What I gave, I have. What I kept, I lost."

Think about it. Our generosity in this life precedes us into eternity. This man invested for eternity. You will never become a significant giver to God's work until you truly understand this principle. Knowing which investments constitute worldly wealth and which constitute true riches will free you to be extravagantly generous. And extravagantly happy.

VIEW EVERY NEED AND DESIRE AS A CHANCE TO TRUST GOD

But how do you integrate a commitment to invest for eternity with a growing spiritual vitality? That brings us to the second Eternal Principle: View every need and desire as a chance to trust God. We see this principle in the Lord's prayer in Matthew 6:11: "Give us today our daily bread."

This kind of mind-set is so foreign to our society. Few of us actually are in a position to trust our heavenly Father for our daily bread. We go to the supermarket, which houses all manner of fruits, vegetables, meat, dairy products, and anything else we might need or want—including every type of bread imaginable—trucked in from mega farms that have perfected the art of feeding the masses.

And truth be told, we usually enjoy this bounty without a second thought. Our sights are usually trained on bigger game. We live in a world of cell phones, satellite TV, flat screens, and lattes. Those are the things we dream about, scheme for, and spend on. Daily bread we take for granted most of the time.

But God says, "No, pray for your daily bread." Why? For one thing, this prayer reminds us where our daily provisions come from. They come from our Provider. And they help us experience Him as such. They also cultivate in us a thankful heart.

But we don't often pray this way, do we? As I've focused on experiencing God as my Provider, for the last several years I've been prompted to pray, "Lord, please give me Your provisions today. Provide the things You want to provide today." Give us this day our daily bread.

And, as we trust God to provide, we can rest assured of His

> *God says, "Pray for your daily bread." Why? For one thing, this prayer reminds us where our daily provisions come from. They come from our Provider.*

answer. As Psalm 34:10 says, "Those who seek the Lord lack no good thing." I have a colleague who was laid off and wondered how he would feed his family. But in the following weeks and months, as he prayed with renewed vigor for his daily bread, he saw God provide food in his refrigerator and cupboards. This man, his wife, and his children have lacked no good thing.

Soaking our minds and hearts in applicable Scriptures is another way to deepen our trust in our Provider—and there are tons of these verses. One that has meant so much to me is Ecclesiastes 2:26: "To the man who pleases him, God gives wisdom, knowledge and happiness, but to the sinner he gives the task of gathering and storing up wealth to hand it over to the one who pleases God."

One of the earliest life-changing experiences I had with experiencing God as my Provider came when I was a young Christian and in my twenties. The consulting firm where I worked had a slow summer and didn't have a lot for me to do, so I took a leave of absence without pay for the summer to volunteer at a Christian camp. At the end of the summer, the camp's leadership and board invited me to join their missionary staff as their director of stewardship and marketing. I accepted the position and took a 90 percent pay cut from the consulting firm. When winter showed up and the snow started to pile up in November in northern Wisconsin, I discovered that the shoes I had weren't warm enough and did not have enough traction for the ice-and-snow-covered dirt roads and walking paths around the camp. So I began to pray to God for money to buy warm winter boots. A few days later I went to my mailbox and there were three letters from friends. I was so excited because I was sure that God had led these friends to send me a letter and put some money in the envelope. But when I opened the letters there was no money inside. I was discouraged. (On a side note, if you ever send a missionary a letter, put some money inside and I know you will be an answer to prayer!) Anyway, I went to my office discouraged.

A while later my friend Larry came up into the office carrying a pair of winter boots. I asked him why he had the boots, and he said that when he bought his house recently that these boots were up in the loft of the barn he now owned. But he said the boots didn't fit him and he was looking for someone who could use a pair of warm winter boots. I quickly said, "Well, I could use some boots." Larry said, "Well here, try these on to see if they fit." When I tried them on I knew how Cinderella felt when she tried on the glass slipper. They fit me perfectly and they were warm too! This is a moment I have never forgotten. Because in that very moment, I learned that God is bigger than money! He can provide the very item you need, when you need it. God doesn't follow the philosophy of actor Tom Cruise in the *Jerry Maguire* sports agent movie, when he shouts, "Show me the money!" When you honor, serve, and follow God in your life, it's not about money, it's about God's provisions.

At any moment, God can choose to bring the resources of the godly and ungodly into our lives. God can choose to "transfer ownership" of something that someone else has to you at a fraction of the cost and sometimes for free. Some people are great shoppers at consignment stores, thrift shops, and garage sales and save 70 percent, 80 percent, and even 95 percent off the original cost of the item. Ecclesiastes 2:26 is the "garage-sale shoppers" life verse—that God will provide the wealth stored up by others to meet their needs.

Another verse like it is Proverbs 13:22: "A sinner's wealth is stored up for the righteous."

Job 27:16–17 has a similar perspective. "Evil people may have piles of money and may store away mounds of clothing. But the righteous will wear that clothing" (NLT).

When I worked at the camp in the northwoods of Wisconsin, sometimes it would get down to minus thirty or forty degrees Fahrenheit in the winter. Many of the staff people would heat their homes with wood. Wood is a wonderful way to keep warm. It heats you five times: when you cut it, when you stack it, when you bring it in, when you burn it, and when you clean out the stove. Staff members would buy huge logs and have them delivered to their homes. Each of us would get the wood dropped off in our yards, and on Thursday mornings in the fall ten to fifteen people would show up at a fellow staffer's house to cut that person's wood for the winter. We had log splitters, chainsaws, and axes. When people arrived at your house, you gave them breakfast; in return, all of your wood got cut, split, and stacked.

Now, if you were smart you bought good oak, because that was the best-burning wood, and if you were really smart you would get it a year ahead. That way it would dry for a whole year and burn really well in the fireplace or wood stove. I was determined to be smart. One year I bought the best oak wood and it sat there for a year, cut, dry, stacked, and ready just as winter started to set in.

At this time there was a staff member who didn't have the money to buy good wood for his family. Winter was starting, snow was coming, his house was cold, and he had to go down to the camp wood shop to rummage for wood scraps.

As Sandi and I wondered how to help his family, our insurance company called and said we couldn't heat with wood anymore. We prayed about what to do with all that beautiful oak, and the solution was obvious. We called our friend and offered it to him. Grateful and excited, he got the camp dump truck and came right over. As he began moving it to his house, he said with a twinkle in his eye, "Hey, Brian, what's that Bible verse you always quote? 'The wealth of the sinner is stored up for the righteous'?"

I said, "Yes, I'm a forgiven sinner and my wealth has been stored up for your righteous need to care for your family!" Our friend knew how to view every need and desire as a chance to trust God—and so did we.

GAIN BIBLICAL UNDERSTANDING

The next Eternal Principle is basic: Gain biblical understanding. "I have hidden your word in my heart," Psalm 119:11 says, "that I might not sin against you." Did you know that there are 2,350 verses in the Bible that deal with finances, material possessions, and generosity? That's a lot! And yet most people know very few of these verses because many pastors and churches shy away from teaching people about what the Bible says about these important subjects. That's one of the reasons I wrote the *40 Day Spiritual Journey to a More Generous Life* Bible devotional and the free www.GiveWithJoy.org eDevotional. These two resources have four hundred Bible verses to help people learn how to manage their finances and giving according to the Bible.

Why do I stress learning God's Word? It's simple, really. Second Timothy 3:16–17 says straightforwardly, "All Scripture is God-breathed and is useful for teaching, rebuking, correcting and training in righteousness, so that the man of God may be thoroughly equipped for every good work." God provides for those who are walking with Him, who are learning His Word and applying it.

A few years ago the banks failed in Mongolia and everyone who had money in the bank lost it. A church contacted me and asked if they could translate my *Generous Life* Bible devotional into Mongolian in order to bring help and hope to the people in their congregation who had lost all their money. I said yes, and they translated it and gave it out to 1,100 Christian believers. The executive pastor emailed me months later and said God's Word in this devotional helped calm people's troubled hearts and the giving at the church increased nearly 60 percent. In Australia, a pastor at a young church plant used this devotional and he gave a testimony at an event where

I was speaking that the giving at their church increased 600 percent after his people realized God wanted them to learn to become generous. In China, one of the largest churches in the country printed eight thousand copies for the members in their church. Leaders in India translated this devotional into eleven Indian languages, and within the next year, Christian leaders in Latin America plan on distributing hundreds of thousands of copies across thirteen countries.

In Indiana, a church was running 20 percent behind their budget. After giving out copies of the *40 Day Generous Life* devotional weekly offerings began increasing 50 to 100 percent each week. Across America over 1,300 churches have given out copies of this Bible devotional to inspire generosity and increase giving.

Why would churches from all over the country and world be distributing this Bible devotional? Because people of every language, culture, and color need to know and follow God's Word on how to manage their finances and giving.

God's principles work. In every country and language group, people need to hear the Word of God on this subject. I've seen God provide for His people all over the world. I've traveled in South America, Europe, Asia, India, Russia, and points in between. I've seen God provide for people whether they have little or much.

The worldly ways of managing your finances will sooner or later bring pain and confusion. You can make a lot of foolish financial decisions very quickly and suffer for a long, long time. But you can avoid that by hiding God's Word in your heart so that you might not sin against Him. As you learn and apply His Eternal Principles, you gain access to the true riches. Your faith becomes stronger and more exciting as you invest for eternity, share your "whatevers" with those in need, view each need and desire as an opportunity to trust God, and hide His Word in your heart.

Where are you in the journey? May you experience God's grace, provision, and love as you apply the Eternal Principles found in His Word.

For groups, classes, or family discussions, choose the most interesting three to five questions to discuss together.

1. Why do you think the wealthy man who experienced a financial downturn could say he did not regret the giving he did (page 128)?
2. Why do you think it would be wise to follow Jesus' instruction to pray for our daily bread?
3. Share a story where you saw God provide for a specific material need you had.
4. Tell about a special treasure you got at a garage sale, yard sale, thrift shop, auction, or clearance rack.
5. Who has most influenced your understanding a application of biblical financial and generosity principles?

PART THREE

*Respond
to God's Plan*

Chapter 9

CHANGE YOUR HEART

We live as ever in uncertain times and quite naturally look for a rock to hold on to. This book is about experiencing God as our Provider in calm times as well as in the midst of the storms of life. I have seen this God work in my life and in the lives of scores of friends, colleagues, and fellow believers. I have told some of their stories and shared the scriptural bedrock on which this kind of life is founded. This is an exciting, hopeful way to live, and our hope is founded upon a God whose orientation is always to care for, bless, and provide for His children.

GIVE YOUR SIN AND RECEIVE
GRACE AND FORGIVENESS

We have seen in the first section of this book that we must recognize God's provisions: our work, income, and resources. The first step in seeing God as Provider is to acknowledge and put to good use what He has already given. In the second section we saw that we should receive His principles: God first, protection from self, positive things we can do, and eternal perspectives to keep in mind.

We have spotted some of the critical milestones on the journey and the principles we need to learn to follow. But ultimately, our security is not in stable finances or a debt-free life, but in a Savior. Jesus says to us, "Follow me." His call is universal and personal, all at the same time.

In this section, I would like to share with you insights that God has given me about how all of us are on a generosity journey with God. We learn to give to God whatever we have in our life, and God graciously and generously pours back into our lives in incredible ways.

Let me explain a little more. The first step in our generosity journey with God begins in a very unusual place, but this step is essential for all that follows. Our journey, you see, starts when we realize that God loves us and when we also realize we're unclean sinners who have missed the mark for the life God created us for. We need to realize that we are sinners who need a Savior and that Jesus is the only One who can pay the price for our sin-debt. So we intentionally in prayer need to "give" our sin to God. What we deserve on our own is condemnation and damnation. But do you know what God pours out on our lives when we "give Him our sin?" We get salvation, liberation, and justification. We get God's love, grace, cleansing, and forgiveness. Wow!

Think about it. Where else can you go with your sin? Does anyone else want it? You can't give it to your spouse, your parents, or your children—though its power can hurt them terribly. You might bring it to counselors or psychiatrists, and they will listen to you, organize it, package it, and give it back to you! They might even put a label on it, name it for you, and tell you who to blame for it—but they cannot take it from you (not that they would want to if they could).

Our journey starts when we realize that God loves us and when we also realize we're unclean sinners who have missed the mark for the life God created us for.

Only Christ alone can deal with our sin and our failures. When we give it to Him, He takes it and pours His amazing love into our hearts. Romans 5:5–8 explains it like this, "God has poured out his love into our hearts by the Holy Spirit, whom he has given us. You see, at just the right time, when we were still powerless, Christ died for the ungodly. . . . But God demonstrates his own love for us in this: While we were still sinners, Christ died for us."

For me, I was a twenty-one-year-old college student when I gave my sin to Christ and received His love and forgiveness. As I have shared in this book, before knowing Christ I was a liar, a thief, a drunkard, and much worse. But I discovered God could be my Provider. He could provide the cleansing, forgiveness, and new life I so desperately needed.

GIVE YOUR HEART AND RECEIVE A NEW LIFE

The Bible teaches that we have sin-sick hearts. Jeremiah 17:9 diagnoses the illness: "The heart is the most deceitful thing there is, and desperately wicked. No one can really know how bad it is!" (TLB). When I came to Christ as my Savior from sin, I also realized I had a sin-sick heart. Then I read Psalm 51:17 that says, "The sacrifice you desire is a broken spirit. You will not reject a broken and repentant heart, O God" (NLT).

Wow again! I could humbly give my sin-stained heart to God and He would accept it. Not only would He accept it, but He promised to be my Provider and give me a brand new heart! In Ezekiel 36:25–27 the Lord says, "I will sprinkle clean water on you, and you will be clean; I will cleanse you from all your impurities and from all your idols. *I will give you a new heart* and put a new spirit in you; I will remove from you your heart of stone and give you a heart of flesh. And I will put my Spirit in you and move you to follow my decrees and be careful to keep my laws" (italics added).

God took my sin, my sin-sick heart, and even my broken life when I gave it to Him. But I also realized that I didn't have a life worth living. I had hurt family, friends, employers, and I had hurt God by my attitude and actions. But then I read John 10:10. Jesus says, "I have come that they might have life, and have it to the full." I read 2 Corinthians 5:17 that said that if "anyone is in Christ, he is a new creation; the old has gone, the new has come!" John 3:16 said He could give me eternal life. Knowing these three things was another wow! moment. I could "give" God my broken life and He would give me abundant life, He would give me a new life, and He would give me eternal life.

Many people reading this book have discovered everything I have just explained in their own lives. But I know that for some, this could be a divine moment when you begin to understand for the first time that what you can give to the Lord Jesus is your sin, your hard heart, and your broken life. When this happens, you can truly experience God as your Provider—the Provider of amazing love, amazing grace, amazing healing, and so much more.

I hope you know Christ in this way. If not, I hope that today is the day that you experience God as your Provider for things much more valuable than money or the things money can buy.

For groups, classes, or family discussions, choose the most interesting questions to discuss together.

1. Who was influencial in your coming to know God's love for you?
2. Share about when you first experienced God's provision of grace and forgiveness.
3. Why do you think that a gift acceptable to God is a broken spirit and a repentant heart (Psalm 51:17)?
4. How does it make you feel that God can take people's sin-sick hearts and give them a brand new heart? Share some of the details (anonymously, if necessary) about someone you know who really needs God to give them a brand-new heart.

Chapter 10

CHANGE
YOUR GIVING

In the last chapter we saw that we must clear our accounts with our holy Creator before we can experience Him as our loving Father. We do that by giving Him our all—primarily our sinful lives, in exchange for His righteousness. It is the best transaction ever. Eternal life, both now and in the future, is our reward. It costs us nothing, because Jesus paid the debt for our sin that we could not pay.

But once we come to know Christ as our Savior, there is a lifetime journey we go through in making Him the Lord of all aspects of our lives. Martin Luther has been credited with the quote that people go through three conversions. Their heads, their hearts, and their pocketbooks—but unfortunately not all at the same time.

GIVE YOUR FINANCES AND RECEIVE
GOD'S WISDOM AND PROVISIONS

For most people, there is a specific point when they give over their finances to God. Sometimes their finances are a real mess and God has a lot of work to do. When I intentionally turned my finances over to God, I had more month than money. I had a large pile of bills, an empty checkbook, and a small paycheck that wouldn't allow me to pay my bills and live for two weeks, much less give to God. But in prayer, I told the Lord, "The way I am doing my finances isn't working. I'm making a mess of things and I'm in a mess. Lord, from this point forward, whenever I get paid, whether it's little or much, the first thing I will do is write out a check for your work of 10 percent or more of my income."

For me it was a "Jacob decision" (Genesis 28:22) that I talked about earlier in the book. I know many others have made a similar decision. Over the years, I met a few people who made this decision but then informed me that "it didn't work." I asked them, "What didn't work?" They would say, "I began to give to God and no checks came in the mail. The windows of heaven weren't opened up for me." Somehow they thought God was supposed to be their magic genie. But as I have worked with people over the years who have made a spiritual decision to turn their finances over to God and to begin to be faithful givers, here is what I find God "gives them in return."

First, He gives them wisdom to not be so foolish with their finances. Gone are the almost daily experiences of wasteful, foolish, impulsive, and even sinful purchases. Second, He gives them the grace to be able to make lifestyle changes so they can live below their means. Third, He stretches their provisions and makes them go further than they've gone in the past. Fourth, He creatively meets their needs. He may or may not supply money to meet their needs, but He may provide the very item they are needing when they need it. Fifth, He helps them understand that it isn't just about giving

God 10 percent or more, but that they are a temporary steward or manager of 100 percent of what God entrusts them with. He helps people live in the reality of Matthew 6:33, which says that God will provide: "Seek first God's kingdom and what God wants. Then all your other needs will be met as well" (NCV).

> I told the Lord, "The way I am doing my finances isn't working. I'm making a mess of things and I'm in a mess."

One of my favorite stories about someone learning to trust God as their Provider with their finances comes from a friend at my church. Nathan had been let go from his job as a body shop manager. He strung together a variety of part-time and freelance projects to help pay the bills. One day he told me that even though they didn't know how they were going to make it every month, there were two things that were anchors in his life. The first thing was that he got up every day and spent time with God and read his Bible. The second thing was that whenever he got any money from any work, he would give at least 10 percent to God. I asked him if he had any unique stories about discovering how God could be his Provider even when he knew that he went into every week not knowing how they were going to make ends meet. He told me a great story of God's provision when his wife was pregnant with their sixth child. They were praying for money and trying to save to buy a van that would seat eight. They already had a van that held seven, but with the new baby coming, they would legally need a van with eight seats. But no extra money was coming in and the savings plan wasn't working either. So Nathan and Janell prayed, "God, we don't need money, we need a van that seats eight."

One day Nathan was over at the salvage yard looking for parts for someone else, and he noticed a van that had been in an accident.

This vehicle looked identical to the van he already owned. It was the same year, same color, same make, same model, same interior, same everything. There was only one difference. When Nathan peered into the van window, he noticed the van had a three-person bench seat where their van had two captain's chairs. He asked how much the bench seat cost and it was only $35. Nathan bought it and went away rejoicing in the fact that God was his Provider. He told me, "We didn't need money to buy a new van. We didn't even need a different van. All we needed was an eighth seat for the new baby and God met our need!"

God met their need, using their own van and someone else's bench seat. The bench seat was the same color, same interior, same fabric, same everything! That's the kind of thing that happens when you learn to honor God with what you have. You receive far more than what you give: You receive God's wisdom and provisions.

GIVE SYSTEMATICALLY
AND SPONTANEOUSLY

Most conversations about giving to God focus on giving 10 percent or more. And I believe that this systematic approach to proportionate giving is vital to your spiritual well-being and ultimate financial stability. But the Bible speaks about both tithes (systematic or "head giving") and offerings (spontaneous or "heart giving"). Don't forget that systematic giving is only part of God's plan for your life. The other part is spontaneous giving. One is all about the head; the other is all about the heart. In systematic giving, you use your head to determine the percentage or amount you are going to faithfully monitor and give. In spontaneous giving God will prompt your heart to give. It may be anything you have. It may be money, it may be possessions. As we have seen, you have resources under your control. At any moment you can expect God to suddenly move in your heart about one of your possessions and say, "Open your hand and give it." Exodus 35:21 says, "Everyone who was willing and *whose heart moved him* came and brought an offering to the Lord for the work on the Tent of Meeting" (italics added). This giving for the Tent of Meeting was not about systematic giving, but instead was a voluntary and spontaneous freewill offering among those whose hearts were moved by God to give.

When I gave my car to the single mother with six children, this was spontaneous "heart giving." God prompted my heart to open my hands and give this family my car. When I wanted to help the Christian brother from Bhutan purchase a computer for his Bible translation work, God prompted my heart to open my hand and give my computer. Once, my wife and I received some inheritance money. In the middle of the night God prompted my heart to give a five-figure gift from this inheritance that was beyond the 10 percent of the inheritance that we had already given away. This gift was more than our year's salary. For three hours I lay in bed being hard-hearted and tight-fisted not wanting to let go of this money. Finally, I woke Sandi up in the middle of the night and told her what I thought God wanted us to do. She said, "I agree with God," and rolled over and went back to sleep! The next day, we gave this spontaneous heart-gift with joy.

> *This is not a law of nature or a magic trick. It's all about our miracle-working God, who has told us about the joy of giving.*

When we learn to systematically give, God gets the glory. When we learn to spontaneously give, God gets the glory again. But please note: *When we give, we don't lose.* Our own lives benefit. Other people benefit. This is not a law of nature or a magic trick. It's all about our miracle-working God, who has told us about the joy of giving. That's the life of faith. That's part of experiencing God as our Provider, learning to live open-handedly in a tight-fisted world.

GIVE YOUR WEALTH AND RECEIVE
A LEGACY AND REWARDS

Now we'll focus on an aspect of our finances that needs some more attention: Giving God our *wealth*. By wealth I mean the things that we accumulate in life, financial and otherwise. We accumulate friendships, relationships, possessions, and many other things.

I think of a friend. "When I got married," he told me, "everything I owned fit in a little Chevy Vega. Seven years, one marriage, and three kids later, it took the biggest U-Haul truck we could rent and seven trips to transport everything we had to our new house! Where did it all come from? Suddenly we had to have this huge house just for all of our stuff."

Yes, there are seasons of life when it is right and good to accumulate. But there are other seasons when God says, "Open your hands. Let Me use your wealth, whatever it is, to bless others. Let it go. You don't need it anymore." You may not realize how much you have, but I suspect you have more than you think. And I know that what you have can benefit others: a relationship, connections, piece of equipment, car, skills, or whatever.

What treasures has God put in your life? Open your hand and spread the wealth.

Do it now, while you have control of it. A lot of people make the mistake of accumulating resources without asking, "When am I going to let them go, and to whom am I going to give them?" As Ecclesiastes 3:1 says, "There is a time for everything, and a season for every activity under heaven." Your fifties and later is a great season to open your hand and begin letting things go.

In addition, be sure to have a giving plan for when you die. Put it in your will and make sure you include the kingdom of God among your beneficiaries. Then you will have a legacy that will outlast you and produce eternal rewards, both for you and others. Deuteronomy 8:18 says, "But remember the Lord your God, for it is he who gives you the ability to produce wealth."

How do we remember God as our Provider? One way is to intentionally return to Him the wealth He gives. I mentioned that Randy Alcorn says that sometimes God increases His provisions not to increase our standard of living, but to increase our standard of giving.

One day a camp director friend of mine got a call from a Christian family. They asked on the phone, "Could the camp use a tractor?"

"We sure can," was the prompt reply.

"How about draft horses?"

"Sure can," my friend responded.

"What about riding horses? . . . Saddles? . . . Cattle? . . . Farm equipment? . . . Horse trolley that seats twenty people?" The answer was yes each time.

My friend then asked, "Why do you want to give all of this to us?" The man replied, "My family is breaking up the family farm. All the siblings have everything they need in life and don't need any more money or any more stuff. We just want our things to be used for the Lord and we know that your camp is doing a great job reaching families and young people for Christ and we want you to have all of this if you can put it to good use."

Now this was a family that understood sharing their wealth for the sake of the kingdom of God and for storing up treasures in heaven.

For groups, classes, or family discussions, choose the most interesting questions to discuss together.

1. Were there any particular milestones in your life when you felt you experienced God's conversion of your head, your heart, and your pocketbook?

2. After you began to be a faithful giver to God's work, what is some wisdom you feel God gave you to make better decisions with your finances?

3. Share some examples from your life about the difference between systematic/head giving and spontaneous/heart giving. Why do you think both are important?

4. What are some possessions you currently have that you no longer use that you could share, give, or sell for kingdom purposes?

Chapter 11

CHANGE
YOUR LIFE

In the last chapter we examined the benefits of turning our finances and wealth over to the Lord. If we give Him our finances, we receive His provisions and wisdom. If we give Him our stored-up wealth, we receive a legacy of generosity and service and His eternal rewards. We concluded with the thought that changing our giving will help us gain our lives, both now and in the future. As Jesus said, "For whoever wants to save his life will lose it, but whoever loses his life for me will find it" (Matthew 16:25). Applied to our financial lives, how is this paradox possible? How do we find our financial life when we are faithful in turning it over to Him? I believe this happens when we make another commitment—turning our lifestyle over to Him.

GIVE YOUR LIFESTYLE TO GOD AND RECEIVE CONTENTMENT AND PEACE

We have to face the fact that, if we are going to live for God our Provider, we will be swimming against the cultural stream. We are urged to accumulate more and more stuff and to build financial protection into our lives so that we can pay for every need imaginable: unexpected bills, college, retirement, a fancy car to lessen the pain of midlife, a vacation home, travel. The culture is never satisfied, and neither are we. It sometimes seems that the more we have, the more we want. When asked once how much money is enough, billionaire John D. Rockefeller is said to have replied, "Just a little bit more." If John D. Rockefeller found it hard to stop the money chase, what hope is there for the rest of us?

> First Timothy 6:6 says, "Godliness with contentment is great gain." It doesn't say winning the lottery is great gain or getting a fancier car or buying a bigger house.

So many people believe the old bumper sticker, "He who dies with the most toys wins." But perhaps we should pay attention to another bumper sticker: "He who dies with the most toys still dies." There is no advantage to being the richest man in the cemetery. As a pastor, I've been to a lot of funerals, but I've never seen a U-Haul behind the hearse. You can't take it with you, but I believe you can send it on ahead.

The German theologian and pastor Dietrich Bonhoeffer who was martyred for his faith in World War II said, "The first call which every Christian experiences is the call to abandon the attachments of this world." True disciples reach a certain place where we say, "We're going to be content in God."

First Timothy 6:6 says, "Godliness with contentment is great gain." It doesn't say winning the lottery is great gain or getting a fancier car or buying a bigger house. It says godliness with contentment is great gain. So that means every person reading this book can have great gain. All it takes is godliness with contentment, regardless of where you live or how little or how much money you have. That's good news!

Hebrews 13:5 says, "Keep your lives free from the love of money and be content with what you have, because God has said, 'Never will I leave you; never will I forsake you.'" We cannot change our lifestyle until we have answered the trust question: Will we choose to trust God as our Provider?

Here's a quiz. Which is the most expensive vehicle to operate per mile? A Maserati? A Mercedes? A BMW? No, it is a shopping cart!

Driving a shopping cart down a store aisle just eighty feet long can cost hundreds of dollars. And yet, if we filled twenty shopping carts with everything we could buy, we wouldn't be any more content. Remember what I shared earlier in the book. Contentment doesn't come from getting everything you want, but from being thankful for everything you have.

A Southern California businessman who swapped his luxury car for a clunker is encouraging others to do the same in order to help spread the gospel. Several years ago Mike Foster, a creative director at a successful design firm, purchased his dream car—a $50,000 Infiniti sports coupe. Then in 2006, Foster traded his luxury car for a 1993 Toyota Camry he calls the "Green Gremlin." Foster now uses the monthly $600 savings to support a Christian ministry.

"Because I gave up that car payment, I'm now taking that money and I am able to sponsor four kids through Compassion International," he shares. "It's just an amazing thing because when I was driving that sports car, it was all about me. [But] when I traded in that sports car, my car then became an opportunity for me

> *In 2006, Foster traded his luxury car for a 1993 Toyota Camry he calls the "Green Gremlin." Foster now uses the monthly $600 savings to support a Christian ministry.*

to have my life be about somebody else and releasing kids from poverty."

Soon Foster began inviting his colleagues and friends to do the same, and now there are more than three thousand members of the Junky Car Club. He explains how straightforward it is. "I run into people all the time, who say, 'Mike, I'd love to support an organization like Compassion, or I'd love to give more to charity, but I just don't have any money at the end of the month.' A great answer and a great way to respond is to ask, 'What about your car? Are you making car payments?' Just to say [to them], 'Let's stop that [type of] thinking and get something that we can afford, that we can pay for outright—and then use that money for charitable means that are out there.'"

The slogan of Junky Car Club—"Living with less so we can give more."

I met a pastor in Costa Rica who was a sweet, gentle man. My wife and I were out for a walk with him one day. This pastor was telling us how God had provided for his every need. This man lived in a simple house, eating beans and rice for breakfast, lunch, and dinner. His vehicle was not a sports car or an SUV. It was an old bicycle. Here was someone displaying both godliness and contentment. He was experiencing great gain, whether he had much of the world's goods, or little. And you know what else he had? True happiness!

"Watch out!" Jesus says in Luke 12:15. "Be on your guard against all kinds of greed; a man's life does not consist in the abundance of his possessions."

A few years ago, I heard a man named Steve from California

speak at a Christian conference. He told the story of how he and his wife became millionaire givers! Steve owned a small business and made about $50,000 a year. He went to a Campus Crusade for Christ conference and heard Dr. Bill Bright challenge everyone in the audience to each give $1 million to the Lord's work. After the message, he went up to Dr. Bright and asked, "Obviously, you didn't really mean that my wife and I should be included in the people who will give a million dollars to the Lord's work?"

Dr. Bright asked, "How much did you make last year?"

Steve said, "$50,000."

Dr. Bright asked him how much he gave to the Lord last year. Steve said, "$15,000."

Steve thought Dr. Bright would be impressed that he gave more than 25 percent of his income to the Lord's work.

Dr. Bright said, "Well, next year, trust God to allow you to give $50,000."

But Steve said, "That's my entire salary!"

Dr. Bright said, "Trust God and if He provides you with the funds, give $50,000!"

Steve went home and amazingly his little business did well and he and his young family lived on their $50,000 salary and they gave $50,000 to the Lord's work! The next year, by faith, they pledged to themselves and the Lord that they would continue to live on $50,000 but would seek to give $100,000 to the Lord's work if God provided it. Amazingly, through some unbelievable circumstances and a great testing of their faith, they were able to give $100,000 that year. Each year, they continued to live on their basic salary and give their extra income to the Lord's work. And believe it or not, within five years, they had given over a million dollars to the Lord!

This is the kind of thing that happens when we learn to cap our lifestyle and give the extra to the Lord. Is this radical? Perhaps, but only if you forget who your Provider is. While the world is ever consumed with money worries, if you lay your lifestyle on God's altar, you can rest assured that He will provide you with contentment and peace. He has for us.

GIVE YOUR INFLUENCE AND
RECEIVE JOY AND FELLOWSHIP

When you experience God as your Provider, giving begins to become as second nature as breathing. God gives all we have, and as we get to know Him better on this journey, we become more like Him. We start to share all of His provisions with those around us. This is about much more than our finances. It is about our lives.

One of God's vital nonmonetary provisions that we share is our influence. God has uniquely equipped us to influence a specific set of people by virtue of our history, gifts, passions, and opportunities.

You don't have to be a pastor or a missionary to share your influence. People in the marketplace can reach folks that the clergy never could. An attorney friend of mine has blessed many people in our church with her willingness to share her influence, ability, knowledge, and understanding of the legal system to help people she knows. To my knowledge, whenever ministers have come to her, she has never charged them for her services. Instead she views helping them as another way to serve the Lord.

Near the end of his life, my dear friend and mentor, John Hedlund, had to go to many physicians. "Lord," John said, "if I'm going to be in the doctor's offices, I want you to use me to be an encouragement to a nurse, a doctor, or somebody sitting in the waiting room." Other friends of ours enjoy going out to restaurants for meals, and they have shared the love of Christ with many waiters and waitresses over the years and led many of them to Christ.

Another friend of ours is a professor of Portuguese at the Air Force Academy. She was going to take about twenty young Air Force cadets on a language-learning experience in Brazil. Finding out that each of the cadets was going to be allowed to bring two suitcases on the plane, she made a plan. Knowing the cadets would pack lightly and would only need one suitcase, Alice made sure that every Air Force Academy cadet brought another packed with fifty pounds of clothes. So, she and her group hand-carried over one thousand pounds of clothes to help needy families in Brazil. When I heard about this, I went through my closet to give her any of the clothes I wasn't regularly wearing.

You've probably heard the credit card commercial slogan, "What's in your wallet?" Well, God asks us, "What's in your closet—and your dresser, garage, basement, and storage unit?" Learn to go through your possessions regularly and give to people or causes what you are no longer using.

Alice has now started a clothes ministry, built a website, and is contacting people who are going on international trips to do the same thing. This ministry doesn't cost a single dollar. It's just people giving clothes they are no longer using, putting them in a suitcase, and giving them to someone on an airplane who will hand them to a Christian worker who will distribute them among needy families. Alice is using her influence and receiving joy and fellowship in return.

I know of a dentist who contacted a Christian camp that had ministered to his family. This man asked if there was any way he could use his dentistry to serve the Lord. Willing to give up time and income to further the kingdom, this dentist ended up providing free care to the twenty camp missionaries and their thirty children. Every week this dentist scheduled one of these fifty people for a dentist appointment to take care of any and all dental needs. He was using his dentist abilities for God's glory and to serve the needs of God's servants at the camp. He loved doing this, and he and his wife received great joy in the relationships they built with all the camp staff and their children.

My friend Andres Panasiuk has spoken to hundreds of thousands of people in countries across Latin America. Andres and

Crown Financial Ministries have trained 300,000 pastors and leaders across the region in the last five years and established relationships with more than 100,000 churches. Andres is excited about the *40 Day Generous Life* devotional I wrote. He is planning to use his influence and connections to spread the use of the *Generous Life* devotional across thirteen countries in Latin America to help inspire generosity and increase giving to churches, outreaches, and missions. He is using his gifts and connections to spread God's Word on generosity.

Find your sphere of influence and begin to look for ways to be a blessing to others. This will bring you greater lasting joy than you'll ever get by getting some new gadget or gizmo. It will also bring you into deeper fellowship and friendship with others. Not only with those you serve, but those you serve with. My greatest and most enduring and enjoyable friendships have come from serving the Lord with other people.

Giving your influence will not only change your life, it will change your future, giving you a unique purpose and destiny. Are you ready to discover your future as one who trusts God as Provider? That's what the next, and final, chapter is all about.

For groups, classes, or family discussions, choose the most interesting three to five questions to discuss together.

1. Why do you think the Bible says, "Godliness with contentment is great gain" (1 Timothy 6:6)? If you actively lived out this verse in your life, what difference do you think it would make?
2. Talk about the wisdom and benefits of the Junky Car Club's slogan of "living with less so we can give more."

3. Why is God's presence better than money and things?
4. What did you think about the story of Steve who capped his lifestyle and spending and ultimately gave a million dollars to God's work?
5. How do you think God could use your role in your workplace or community to influence people for good and for God?

Chapter 12

CHANGE
YOUR FUTURE

Although I don't know what your past and present has been, I know what your future can be if you allow God to weave the scriptural truths in this book into the fabric of your life. When my family went on a short-term mission trip to Costa Rica last year, we visited a tall bridge that overlooked two rivers that merged under the bridge. On one side of the bridge you saw the two rivers. One river had clear water and the other river had bright yellow water that came from the golden rocks and minerals higher up in the rain forest jungles. On the other side of the bridge the rivers now merged into one river and there was a merging of the colors that now created a new golden river.

By God's grace, He has used this book to bring our lives

together. You have your life, your stories, and your history. Now God has joined you with my life, my favorite Scriptures, my stories, and my history. And now your future can look different on the other side of the bridge.

Based on the Bible and my journey with the Lord that has been outlined in this book, here are some things I desire for your future that I know are possible with God's help, regardless of your age, income, work, or education.

1. You would recognize God as Your Provider, and you would "see" His provisions in your life's journey. Hopefully this book has been used by God to ignite your faith in His ability to provide.

2. You would become more and more generous as you excel in the grace of giving. May you be someone who operates on the four S's of joyful, faithful, and generous giving the rest of your life: "Seeing" God's provisions in your life, "Setting aside" unto the Lord what you are going to give, "Systematically" giving what you've set aside, and "Spontaneously" being open-handed and giving when God prompts your heart.

3. You would experience true financial freedom. Financial freedom is not about a set amount of money stored up somewhere; instead it is about building your life on biblical financial principles and trusting God to guide you and provide for you all the days of your life.

4. You would have greater contentment than ever before. May you be someone like my friend from India who is "rich in Christ," because you are thankful for everything you have.

5. You would move toward avoiding and eliminating indebtedness and become debt free. This is truly possible, and it is an incredible way to live.

6. You would become fearless and filled with faith regardless of what happens to the economy, your job, your company, or your pension because you know and live in the confidence that God is *your* Provider.

7. You would have harmony in your family in regard to financial matters. While many marriages and families fight over financial issues, may you and your family be marked by God's peace, wisdom, and guidance.

8. You would experience God's creative provisions in a way that you know that God loves you and cares about you and knows all the details of your life.

9. You would be free to be the person who God wants you to be and to do the things God wants you to do because you are not burdened down and entangled with worldly concerns and the shackles of debt.

10. You would someday experience eternal rewards and relationships for your service and generosity in this life. Jesus said in Luke 16:9, "I tell you, use worldly wealth to gain friends for yourselves, so that when it is gone, you will be welcomed into eternal dwellings." Your generosity in this life that will reach across the street, across the city, across the country, or across the world can be used by God to touch people's lives. And like the famous song "Thank You" by Ray Boltz describes, you will be greeted in heaven by people who were touched by your generosity.

So may you be a person who lives out the truth of John 10:10 where Jesus says that He has come to give you life "to the full."

Each of us has been uniquely created in Christ for good works (Ephesians 2:10). And when we truly give ourselves to God and live for Him and others, we will discover the purpose and destiny we have been created for, which we could never have found when we were living for ourselves. As Paul said, "No eye has seen, no ear has heard, no mind has conceived what God has prepared for those who love him" (1 Corinthians 2:9).

Living with God as our Provider puts God in the center in everything we do, everything we have, and everything we are. We gratefully accept His provisions—material, financial, relational, spiritual—as we seek to honor Him with our lives and abide in His love.

We need to listen anew to His voice and look afresh at His loving mercy. 'I know the plans I have for you,' declares the Lord, "plans to prosper you and not to harm you, plans to give you hope and a future'" (Jeremiah 29:11).

As a final encouragement, I would like to share some of my "God is my Provider" and generosity journey with you. As I mentioned, after serving for ten years as senior pastor at First Evangelical Free Church in Colorado Springs, the leaders and congregation realized God was blessing and expanding my generosity and financial ministry. My *Generous Life* Bible devotional had become a bestseller with hundreds of thousands of copies in print, translations under way in more than forty languages, and an eDevotional and audio version available on radio stations across the country through the www.GiveWithJoy.org radio stories. More speaking requests for leadership conferences and churches began to come in and my www.MAXIMUMgenerosity.org website and free church giving eNewsletter were serving thousands of pastors/leaders across America and in over 150 countries.

It was obvious that I couldn't keep my full-time duties as senior pastor and manage the growing generosity ministry. So, after months of prayer and planning, the church leaders created a position for me to become a full-time Generosity Minister-at-Large to the body of Christ from my church. Their goal was to empower me to help ignite people's faith, inspire generosity, and increase giving across America and around the world. Applying the teaching they had learned from my ministry, they determined that since

I had been a blessing to them for ten years, they would open their hands and share me with the world. They would then search for a new senior pastor.

There was only one catch.

We agreed that my pastor's salary would go to the new senior pastor and I would become a $1-per-year employee of the church. The church would allow donations to come in for my ministry, and my family would continue to receive medical benefits. After the vote at the church business meeting to approve this arrangement, a good friend came up to me. This friend said, with an earnest look on his face, that he didn't want me, my wife, and three teenage children to worry about money. My friend said he was going to personally underwrite our new full-time ministry. Then, with a smile on his face, he handed me . . . a $1 bill. Needless to say, we had a good laugh together. While it was a light moment, I have to admit to some fears about our step of faith. But then I remembered the practice of "counting our blessings" every Sunday night that my wife and I had done in the early years of our marriage. For a number of years, we hadn't done this, but instead just regularly gave 20 to 50 percent or more of our income and blessings to the Lord's work.

So Sandi and I, knowing we were no longer going to have any regular income, began to "count our blessings" again and then set aside money to give to the Lord's work. This is what we have experienced: Every Monday morning we don't know how God will provide for the coming week, but at the start of the week we review what God has graciously and generously provided during the last seven days. And what He provides always surprises and encourages us as we take time to look back. Here's a partial list of how we've experienced God as our Provider in recent months.

- My wife, Sandi, has had a life-threatening cancer for over seven years and had to be put on oxygen 24/7. We needed to buy some expensive medical equipment that wasn't covered by insurance. When Sandi went to purchase the equipment, she discovered a recently reconditioned piece of the same equipment. She was able to buy it for 75 percent off the price of a new one.

- One of our cars was in the shop for repairs. A mechanic told us we needed an additional, unexpected repair for $500. We declined the extra work and asked a mechanic friend to check out the problem. Imagine our reaction when we learned that the "problem" could be fixed by just tightening a screw!

- One day while I was speaking at a church, someone in the congregation heard that I was a $1-a-year employee for my congregation. This person, who didn't know me, put an $1,100 check in the offering plate with a memo, saying, "For 1,100 years of Brian's generosity ministry."

- Every week, churches and individuals place orders for my generosity materials. Although we never know if or when any orders will come in, nearly every week we are amazed that over 1,300 churches have ordered copies of my *Generous Life* devotional for every family in the congregation.

- At a ladies event Sandi won over $100 in door prizes for our kitchen. A week later at a pastor's luncheon, I won the grand prize drawing for a free radio teaching program that was worth a few thousand dollars on one of our local Christian radio stations.

- Recently, one of my computer's external hard drives failed. The technicians told us the repair bill would be $400. After spending many hours unsuccessfully trying to fix the problem, they unexpectedly decided not to charge us for their time. We were grateful for their unexpected generosity.

- A radio network agreed to play my GiveWithJoy.org radio stories on its two hundred stations. The normal charge would have been $42,000, but they decided to play my radio stories for free.

- A Christian businessman offered to pay the $5,000 in costs to help me produce online videos to train pastors and Christian leaders in America and in nearly two hundred countries around the world. The online seminars teach leaders to see God as their Provider and how they can be used by God to help people become more generous and joyful givers.
- My teenage son's iPod wasn't working, so we took it for repair to the retail store. The repairman we worked with decided to fix it for free. As we were preparing to leave, he also handed my son a $30 pair of headphones for free.

As we've counted up these weekly blessings, we have set aside funds in a special account to give to the Lord's work. With our "Blessings Fund," here are some of the things we have been able to do recently:

✓ Faithfully give to our church as our number-one priority.
✓ Provide Bibles for poor Christians in Malawi, Africa.
✓ Give to a ministry worker in Serbia.
✓ Provide money for renovations at our church.
✓ Take visitors out to lunch after church.
✓ Provide donated materials for a Christian radio station.
✓ Send *40 Day* devotional books to a church that gives them to needy people in their community along with bags of food.
✓ Give generously to a camp ministry.
✓ Give away thousands of copies of our *40 Day* devotional away to denominations and ministries who agreed to give a copy to every church pastor in their denomination or network.
✓ Pay for milk to be delivered for a year to a single mother with six children whose husband is in prison.
✓ Help a family in our church meet some medical needs.
✓ Give computer equipment to a ministry in Eastern Europe.

✓ Provide funding for a ministry that is reaching the homeless in our community.

✓ Make generosity online training videos and downloadable materials available to thousands of leaders in two hundred countries free of charge through the www.GlobalGeneros ity.org website.

✓ Provide funding for a ministry in Romania that is reaching thousands of children in Gypsy villages.

✓ Support a ministry in Central America that will provide clean drinking water to ten thousand people.

✓ And much, much more.

And all of this is happening with an annual salary of $1, starting every Monday morning with no guaranteed income promised to us, and not knowing how God will provide for us in the next seven days.

When you learn to trust God as your Provider and then generously and faithfully share whatever He entrusts to you, everything changes. Your life changes, your future changes, your attitude changes, your buying changes, your giving changes. Instead of being gripped by fear, our hearts are filled with faith in God to provide. He can and will do the same for you if you will let Him.

When God becomes your Provider and you become a faithful and generous giver, your life is different. Something else also changes. Eternity will be different. Those you touch with your generosity will be drawn into a closer relationship with God. Every generous act you ever do, no matter how small, will be recorded, remembered, and rewarded by God. In Matthew 10:42, Jesus says, "And if anyone gives even a cup of cold water to one of these little ones because he is my disciple, I tell you the truth, he will certainly not lose his reward." Hebrews 6:10 points out, "For God is not unjust. He will not forget how hard you have worked for him and how you have shown your love to him by caring for other believers, as you still do" (NLT).

Experiencing God as your Provider, you will no longer fear what the world fears, or crave what the world craves. You will stop grasping at things that don't last and open your hand. Awaiting your treasure in heaven, you will also enjoy God's provisions now. You will have the best of both worlds—God now and God forever.

Do not store up for yourselves treasures on earth, where moth and rust destroy, and where thieves break in and steal. But store up for yourselves treasures in heaven, where moth and rust do not destroy, and where thieves do not break in and steal. For where your treasure is, there your heart will be also (Matthew 6:19–21). AMEN.

For groups, classes, or family discussions, choose the most interesting three to five questions to discuss together.

1. On the list of ten things on pages 164–167, what one or two things do you really desire for your life in the future?
2. What steps do you need to take iin order to practice the four S's of living a generous life (Seeing God's provisions, Setting aside for the Lord, Systematic giving, and Spontaneous giving?
3. If you have any indebtedness, what active steps can you take to eliminate this debt in the next year, three years, ten years?
4. What are some thoughts you had when you read the "blessings" list and giving items on pages 168–169?
5. What do you feel is the most important life-changing truth that God has taught you through reading this book? How do you think this will impact your choices, lifestyle, and giving in the future?

ACKNOWLEDGMENTS

A book project is a team effort and I want to express my deepest appreciation to the Moody Publishers staff whose help, direction, encouragement, expertise, and labors have helped put this book into your hands. I would also like to acknowledge Stan Guthrie, who took the "Experience God as Your Provider" sermons I preached at my church and turned them into a book that you could enjoy.

Additional Resources by
Brian Kluth

www.GodIsYourProvider.com

Find many audio and video messages and seminars of Brian Kluth teaching on the subject of this book. Church and small group/class resources are also available. Order copies of the book in print, eBook, iPad, or Kindle versions. Quantity discounts are available for small groups, classes, churches, ministries, and businesses.

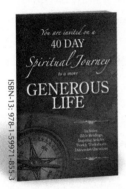

ISBN-13: 978-1-59971-855-3

40 Day Bible Devotional—
www.GenerousLife.org

This bestselling devotional has inspired thousands to learn to live generously. Over 1,300 churches have given out copies to every family in their congregation to ignite faith, inspire generosity, and increase giving. A 40-Day church campaign kit with videos, banners, posters, children's material, sermon helps, and much more is also available. Translations are under way or available in over forty languages.

Radio—www.GiveWithJoy.org Online eDevotional

This FREE online eDevotional is based on the popular *40-Day Generous Life* book. The daily email includes: Bible readings, audio teaching, cartoon, radio stories about people's generosity journey, and weekly discussion questions. Hundreds of radio stations play the free www.GiveWithJoy.org 60-second radio stories for their listening audience. Many churches and ministries include a link to this free eDevotional on their website.

Additional Resources by Brian Kluth

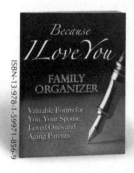

Organizer—www.MyFamilyForms.org

Brian spent two years researching and writing the *Because I Love You Family Organizer.* This manual is filled with more than forty forms to help families better organize their household, shopping, family history, life stories, finances, and funeral/estate wishes. Many churches, professionals, and ministries give out this tool as an affordable gift.

Churches—www.MAXIMUMgenerosity.org

This website for pastors and churches has hundreds of articles, stewardship products, and helpful resources to inspire biblical generosity and increase church giving. A FREE eNewsletter is sent to thousands of pastors and church leaders across America and 150 countries.

Research—www.STATEofthePLATE.info

Brian conducts annual research with Christianity Today International on church giving and personal finances/giving. News stories about this research have appeared in the *Wall Street Journal, Washington Times,* ABC, CBS, NBC, Fox, Associated Press, National Public Radio, and major newspapers and magazines around the world.

A Revolution in Generosity

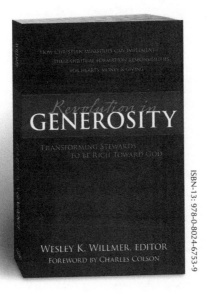

ISBN-13: 978-0-8024-6753-9

A Revolution in Generosity is a work by some of the best scholars and practitioners on the subject of funding Christian organizations. As Wesley Willmer writes, "The foundation for realizing a revolution in generosity is understanding the biblical view of possessions, generosity, and asking for resources." With over twenty expert contributors, this book is a must-read for organizations striving to rid themselves of secular asking practices and gain an eternal approach.

MOODY
PUBLISHERS
www.MoodyPublishers.com

Debt-Free Living

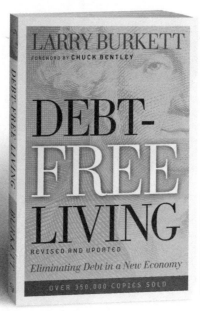

ISBN-13: 978-0-8024-2566-9

With credit, mortgages, car payments, salaries, commissions, and bills fluctuating daily, *Debt-Free Living* has never looked more attractive. This bestselling book has been updated and revised to reflect today's realities alongside timeless biblical truth. Learn about the origin of most financial troubles and break out of the debt cycle. *Debt-Free Living* is a necessary resource to battle the ever-present temptation and trappings of more and more debt that keep weighing you down.

MOODY
PUBLISHERS
www.MoodyPublishers.com